How to Become Financially Free in 30 Days

How to Become Financially Free in 30 Days

10,000 PATHS TO PROSPERITY

Matthew Petchinsky

Apophis Enterprises LLC

1

How to Become Financially Free in 30 Days: 10,000 Paths to Prosperity
By: Matthew Petchinsky

Chapter 1: The Financial Freedom Mindset
Introduction to the Concept of Financial Freedom:
In this initial chapter, the journey toward financial freedom begins by understanding its core principles. Financial freedom isn't simply the absence of debt or the ability to retire early; it's a state of mind where your finances enable you to live life on your own terms. It's about having enough wealth and passive income streams to sustain your lifestyle and meet your goals without feeling financially constrained. This means you have control over your financial future, and your money is working for you rather than the other way around.

To lay the foundation, the chapter provides a comprehensive explanation of financial independence and how it differs from simply being "debt-free." It distinguishes between various stages of financial freedom, from achieving stability, through accumulating wealth, to ultimately attaining true freedom. Each level requires a shift in mindset and strategic financial behavior.

Key highlights include:

- **Defining Financial Freedom:** A personalized and holistic interpretation of what it means for different people.
- **Stages of Financial Independence:** From being debt-free to accumulating wealth and living independently from active income.
- **Benefits of Financial Freedom:** The security, opportunities, and lifestyle flexibility that come with it.

Psychological Barriers to Financial Success and How to Overcome Them:
Achieving financial freedom is not just a matter of income or investment; it requires a profound shift in mindset. Many people unknowingly hold beliefs and attitudes that hinder their financial success, such as fear of failure, scarcity thinking, and undervaluing their worth. These subconscious barriers can limit our potential and keep us stuck in unfulfilling financial patterns.

This section identifies and deconstructs some of the most common psychological barriers:

- **Scarcity Mindset:** A belief that resources are limited and that life is a zero-sum game where another's gain is your loss. This can lead to a defensive, risk-averse attitude.
- **Fear of Failure:** A crippling fear that mistakes will lead to disaster, preventing people from taking calculated financial risks.
- **Self-Limiting Beliefs:** Internalized beliefs like "I don't deserve wealth" or "I'm not good with money" that can stifle one's drive to succeed.

Overcoming these barriers requires intentional psychological work:

- **Abundance Mindset:** Encourages viewing the world as a place of unlimited opportunity where there is more than enough for everyone. It promotes collaboration and creative thinking.
- **Positive Visualization:** Regularly visualizing specific financial goals to reprogram the subconscious mind, thus aligning daily behavior with those objectives.
- **Self-Education and Empowerment:** Gaining financial literacy and understanding money management tools helps build confidence and dispel myths around financial inadequacy.

This chapter concludes by emphasizing that cultivating the right mindset is the first crucial step on the path to financial freedom. Breaking through mental barriers and developing positive beliefs will form the psychological foundation for the strategies detailed in the upcoming chapters.

Chapter 2: Financial Planning Basics
Understanding Your Current Financial Status:

To embark on the journey to financial freedom, it's vital to take an honest and comprehensive look at your current financial situation. Knowing where you stand financially is the starting point for creating a plan that can lead to prosperity. This section walks readers through a step-by-step assessment of their finances:

1. **Net Worth Calculation:**
   - **Assets:** A thorough inventory of all assets, including cash, investments, properties, and other valuables. The chapter provides guidance on how to accurately value less-liquid assets.
   - **Liabilities:** A detailed examination of all debts, loans, and financial obligations, from credit cards and student loans to mortgages and other long-term debt.
   - **Net Worth Formula:** Assets minus liabilities, giving a clear picture of one's financial standing.
2. **Income and Expenses Analysis:**
   - **Income Sources:** List all income streams, including wages, side businesses, and passive investments. This is crucial to understand monthly cash flow.
   - **Expense Breakdown:** Track spending across categories like housing, food, transportation, and entertainment. Identifying patterns and non-essential expenses can reveal potential savings.
3. **Emergency Fund Check:**

- Assess the size and availability of emergency savings. The chapter stresses the importance of having 3-6 months of expenses in an accessible account.

4. **Debt Structure Review:**
   - Identify high-interest debts versus manageable loans. The chapter recommends prioritizing debts that erode financial health the most.

5. **Credit Score and History Analysis:**
   - Learn how your credit score affects borrowing potential and how to access and analyze credit reports to identify potential issues.

Setting Realistic Financial Goals:

With a clear understanding of current finances, the next step is setting realistic and motivating financial goals. The chapter provides a framework for establishing goals that are Specific, Measurable, Achievable, Relevant, and Time-bound (SMART):

1. **Short-Term Goals (1-2 Years):**
   - **Debt Reduction:** Develop targeted strategies to eliminate credit card and other high-interest debts.
   - **Emergency Fund Expansion:** If underfunded, set a goal to build up a 3-6 month emergency savings account.
   - **Major Purchases:** Plan for significant expenses like a car, vacation, or education.

2. **Medium-Term Goals (3-5 Years):**
   - **Down Payment for Property:** Start saving for a home or rental property investment.
   - **Career and Education Advancement:** Allocate funds for courses or certifications to boost career prospects.

3. **Long-Term Goals (5+ Years):**
   - **Retirement Planning:** Develop a clear strategy to build a retirement nest egg, incorporating employer-sponsored plans, IRAs, and investment strategies.

- **Financial Independence Fund:** Work toward generating passive income streams that can sustain your lifestyle independent of full-time employment.

Goal Implementation Strategies:

- **Budgeting:** Create a realistic budget to meet your goals while still living comfortably. Learn about various budgeting techniques like zero-based budgeting or the 50/30/20 rule.
- **Automating Savings:** Set up automatic transfers to savings and investment accounts to ensure consistent progress.
- **Investment Plans:** Explore investment vehicles aligned with your goals, risk tolerance, and time horizon.

By the end of this chapter, readers will have a clear assessment of their current financial standing and a set of achievable, inspiring goals to move forward with confidence. The financial plan developed here will serve as the blueprint for the remaining chapters, where we explore various strategies and paths to achieve these goals in practical, actionable ways.

Chapter 3: Budgeting for Success
Techniques for Effective Budgeting:

Budgeting is the cornerstone of financial planning, providing a disciplined framework to align spending with goals. While the concept is simple, implementing a sustainable budget requires thoughtful strategy. In this section, readers will learn various budgeting techniques, each offering unique advantages:

1. **Zero-Based Budgeting:**
   - **Principle:** Every dollar is assigned a purpose, ensuring that income is fully allocated to expenses, savings, or debt reduction.
   - **Implementation:** Start from scratch each month by planning expenditures based on expected income and prioritizing needs over wants.
   - **Benefits:** Offers complete control and accountability, reducing wasteful spending and encouraging mindful allocation.
2. **50/30/20 Rule:**
   - **Principle:** Divide after-tax income into three broad categories: needs (50%), wants (30%), and savings or debt (20%).
   - **Application:** Differentiate between needs (rent, groceries) and wants (entertainment, dining out). Regularly adjust the percentages to reflect changes in goals or circumstances.
   - **Benefits:** Provides flexibility while ensuring sufficient savings, ideal for those new to budgeting.
3. **Envelope System:**
   - **Principle:** Allocate physical cash or digital "envelopes" for specific expense categories (e.g., groceries, transportation).
   - **Execution:** Withdraw or transfer funds into separate envelopes or accounts, limiting each category's spending to its budget.

- **Benefits:** Effective for controlling discretionary spending and building financial discipline.

4. **Reverse Budgeting (Pay Yourself First):**
    - **Principle:** Prioritize savings or investments first, then allocate remaining funds for bills and discretionary spending.
    - **Application:** Automate transfers to investment and savings accounts immediately after payday.
    - **Benefits:** Forces consistent saving and investment growth, especially useful for those with fluctuating incomes.

5. **Value-Based Budgeting:**
    - **Principle:** Allocate spending in alignment with core values and life goals, focusing on quality over quantity.
    - **Execution:** Identify and eliminate expenses that don't align with your priorities while maximizing spending on experiences or items that bring fulfillment.
    - **Benefits:** Fosters a positive relationship with money, reducing guilt around spending and helping develop financial mindfulness.

Tools and Apps to Track Spending:

Modern technology offers countless tools to simplify budgeting and spending tracking. From basic spreadsheets to sophisticated software, each has unique features catering to different preferences and needs:

1. **Spreadsheets (Google Sheets/Excel):**
    - **Customization:** Create tailored templates to track income, expenses, and goals.
    - **Manual Control:** Requires manual entry but allows for complete data customization and formula creation.
    - **Analysis:** Build custom graphs and pivot tables to gain insights into spending trends.
2. **Mobile Budgeting Apps:**
    - **Mint:** Automatically categorizes bank transactions, provides

alerts for bills and overspending, and gives tailored financial advice.

- ○ **YNAB (You Need A Budget):** Focuses on proactive budgeting, assigning each dollar a purpose while encouraging saving for future goals.
- ○ **PocketGuard:** Connects to bank accounts to provide a comprehensive overview of spending, suggesting ways to curb expenses.

3. **Desktop Software:**
   - ○ **Quicken:** Offers powerful features for tracking multiple accounts, managing investments, and planning for retirement.
   - ○ **Personal Capital:** Combines budgeting with robust investment analysis tools, ideal for wealth management.

4. **Banking Apps:**
   - ○ Most banks and credit unions offer apps with built-in budgeting features, enabling customers to categorize transactions, set spending limits, and receive alerts.

5. **Spending Trackers:**
   - ○ **GoodBudget:** An electronic version of the envelope system, allowing users to distribute their budget into digital envelopes.
   - ○ **EveryDollar:** Encourages zero-based budgeting, providing a straightforward interface to plan and monitor expenses.

Choosing the Right Tools:

- Select a tool that matches your financial situation and technical comfort level.
- Trial multiple apps or systems to find one that you can consistently maintain.
- Consider syncing multiple tools (e.g., using an app for daily tracking and spreadsheets for long-term planning).

By combining effective budgeting techniques with the right tools, readers can gain clarity and control over their finances. This chapter emphasizes the importance of proactive budgeting, cultivating a disciplined approach that minimizes stress and allows the freedom to pursue financial goals confidently.

Chapter 4: Emergency Funds and Financial Safety
Importance of an Emergency Fund:
Financial safety hinges on preparing for the unexpected. Whether it's a medical emergency, job loss, or sudden home repair, an emergency fund acts as a financial cushion, preventing these surprises from derailing your financial goals. Here's why an emergency fund is crucial:

1. **Immediate Financial Security:**
   - It provides a ready source of liquid cash to cover immediate expenses without resorting to high-interest credit or disruptive borrowing.

2. **Prevents Debt Accumulation:**
   - Without an emergency fund, individuals often rely on credit cards or personal loans, accumulating debt that becomes a financial burden.

3. **Protects Investments:**
   - Selling long-term investments prematurely to meet short-term needs can disrupt financial growth. An emergency fund ensures your investment strategy stays intact.

4. **Stress Reduction:**
   - Financial uncertainty is a significant source of stress. Having a safety net eases this burden, helping maintain mental health during challenging times.

5. **Enables Financial Growth:**
   - When unexpected expenses are handled smoothly, you're able to stay focused on growing wealth and pursuing long-term financial plans.

Steps to Build and Manage Your Fund:
Building a solid emergency fund requires discipline and strategic planning. Follow these steps to create and manage an effective fund:

1. **Set a Clear Savings Target:**
   - **Amount:** Aim to save 3-6 months of living expenses. Start with a smaller target, like one month's expenses, and gradually increase.
   - **Customize:** Adjust the goal based on personal circumstances like family size, job stability, and lifestyle.

2. **Create a Separate Savings Account:**
   - **High-Yield Savings Account:** Choose an account with high interest and no or minimal withdrawal penalties. Online savings accounts often offer competitive rates.
   - **Accessibility:** Ensure the account remains easily accessible in emergencies while remaining separate from daily spending accounts.

3. **Automate Contributions:**
   - Automate monthly or biweekly transfers from your checking account to the emergency fund. Automating ensures consistent growth without relying on willpower.

4. **Cut Back and Reallocate:**
   - Identify discretionary spending that can be reduced temporarily and funnel these savings into your emergency fund.
   - **Bonus/Tax Refund Allocation:** Redirect windfalls like bonuses or tax refunds toward building the fund.

5. **Supplement with Side Income:**
   - Consider freelance work, part-time gigs, or selling unused items to generate extra income specifically for the fund.

6. **Gradual Scaling:**
   - Start with smaller milestones (e.g., one-month expenses), and increase incrementally to reach the full target. Celebrate small victories to maintain motivation.

7. **Maintenance and Replenishment:**
   - **Reassess Regularly:** Review and adjust the fund every few months to reflect lifestyle changes or new financial goals.
   - **Replenish:** If funds are withdrawn for an emergency, replenish them as soon as possible.

8. **Avoid Misuse:**
   - Clearly define what qualifies as an emergency and resist the urge to dip into the fund for non-essentials.
9. **Combine with Insurance:**
   - Ensure your emergency fund works hand-in-hand with insurance policies like health, home, or unemployment insurance. Proper insurance can minimize the need to dip into the fund.

Emergency Fund Alternatives:

In some cases, additional options can complement or enhance your emergency fund:

1. **Home Equity Line of Credit (HELOC):**
   - A HELOC can offer emergency borrowing at a lower interest rate compared to credit cards, though it requires home equity as collateral.
2. **Retirement Account Loans:**
   - Loans from retirement accounts like a 401(k) can provide short-term emergency cash but have tax implications and repayment requirements.
3. **Cash-Value Life Insurance:**
   - Policies like whole life insurance can provide loans against the accumulated cash value.

Conclusion: By establishing a well-planned emergency fund, you protect yourself against financial disruptions, providing peace of mind and the flexibility to navigate life's uncertainties. This safety net allows you to pursue financial freedom with greater confidence and resilience, staying focused on long-term wealth-building strategies.

Chapter 5: Debt Management Strategies
Overview of Common Debts:

Managing debt is a crucial step toward financial freedom. To tackle debt effectively, one must understand its various forms, implications, and strategies to handle each type.

1. **Credit Card Debt:**
   - **Nature:** Often unsecured and carries high-interest rates, making it challenging to pay off if left unchecked.
   - **Impact:** Monthly interest can quickly accumulate, creating a cycle that prevents principal reduction. Over-reliance on credit cards can also hurt credit scores.
   - **Minimum Payments:** Only paying minimums leads to prolonged repayment periods and significant interest.

2. **Student Loans:**
   - **Federal Loans:** Have fixed interest rates and various repayment options. They offer deferment, forbearance, and income-driven repayment plans.
   - **Private Loans:** Usually variable rates with stricter terms. Lack of government protections makes them riskier and potentially costlier.
   - **Long-Term Impacts:** Failure to manage student loans can affect credit scores, housing prospects, and employment opportunities.

3. **Mortgage Debt:**
   - **Nature:** Secured debt tied to real estate, usually carrying relatively low interest but for a long term (15-30 years).
   - **Types:** Fixed-rate (consistent interest rate) and adjustable-rate mortgages (variable rates that fluctuate with market conditions).
   - **Strategic Management:** Accelerating payments can save

substantial interest over time, while refinancing may offer lower rates.

4. **Auto Loans:**
   - **Nature:** Secured loans tied to vehicles with moderate interest rates and shorter repayment terms.
   - **Depreciation Impact:** Cars depreciate quickly, often resulting in owing more than the vehicle's worth.
   - **Refinancing Risks:** Refinancing to lower monthly payments can extend the loan term and increase the total interest paid.

5. **Personal Loans:**
   - **Unsecured:** Usually obtained for consolidating other debts or covering unexpected expenses. Interest rates vary based on credit scores and lender terms.

Methods to Reduce and Eliminate Debt:

To achieve financial freedom, systematically reducing and eliminating debt is essential. Here are effective strategies for each debt type:

1. **Debt Snowball Method:**
   - **Principle:** Pay off the smallest debt first while maintaining minimum payments on other debts.
   - **Psychological Benefit:** Small wins build momentum, reinforcing commitment to debt reduction.

2. **Debt Avalanche Method:**
   - **Principle:** Pay off the highest-interest debt first to reduce total interest payments.
   - **Mathematical Benefit:** Minimizes the overall interest paid over time.

3. **Debt Consolidation:**
   - **Consolidation Loan:** Combine multiple debts into a single loan with lower interest and a fixed term. This simplifies payments and potentially reduces interest.
   - **Balance Transfer Credit Cards:** Transfer high-interest

debt to a card offering 0% APR for an introductory period. Ensure full repayment before the interest resets.

4. **Income-Driven Repayment Plans (Student Loans):**
   - **Federal Options:** PAYE, REPAYE, IBR, and ICR plans tailor payments to a percentage of discretionary income.
   - **Loan Forgiveness Programs:** Public Service Loan Forgiveness (PSLF) and income-driven plans offer forgiveness after qualifying payments.

5. **Refinancing:**
   - **Student Loans:** Refinancing private loans can reduce interest rates for qualified borrowers. However, it can also reduce repayment flexibility.
   - **Mortgage Loans:** Refinancing to lower rates or different terms can yield significant interest savings.
   - **Auto Loans:** Refinancing can lower monthly payments, especially for those who have improved their credit scores.

6. **Automate Payments:**
   - Set up automatic payments to ensure consistent debt reduction. Many lenders offer interest rate reductions for automated payments.

7. **Increase Income:**
   - Consider side gigs or freelance work to create additional cash flow directed solely toward debt reduction.

8. **Lifestyle Adjustments:**
   - Temporarily reduce discretionary spending (vacations, dining out) to free up funds for debt repayment.
   - Downsize or relocate to reduce fixed expenses like housing.

9. **Debt Settlement or Negotiation:**
   - Work directly with creditors to negotiate better terms or a lump-sum settlement. Be cautious of debt settlement companies that charge excessive fees.

10. **Professional Help:**

- **Credit Counseling:** Non-profit agencies can help with budgeting and negotiating repayment plans.
- **Bankruptcy Advice:** In extreme cases, consult a bankruptcy attorney to explore debt discharge options.

By applying these strategic debt management techniques, readers can take control of their financial future and pave the way to financial freedom. A disciplined approach to paying down debt is crucial to reducing financial stress and reallocating funds toward savings, investments, and long-term prosperity.

Chapter 6: The Freelance Revolution
How to Identify Profitable Freelancing Opportunities:
The rise of the digital economy has paved the way for the freelancing revolution, providing countless individuals with the opportunity to generate flexible income streams. This chapter explores practical steps to identify profitable freelancing opportunities.

1. **Assess Your Skills and Interests:**
   - **Skill Inventory:** Start by listing marketable skills such as writing, graphic design, programming, digital marketing, and more. Include both professional and personal abilities.
   - **Passion Alignment:** Evaluate which skills align with your passions to ensure long-term motivation and commitment.
2. **Market Research:**
   - **Demand Analysis:** Investigate which skills are in high demand by browsing freelancing platforms (Upwork, Fiverr), job boards, and LinkedIn.
   - **Industry Trends:** Follow emerging trends in freelancing fields such as e-commerce, tech consulting, content creation, and data analysis.
   - **Competition Review:** Identify competitors offering similar services and analyze their strengths and pricing.
3. **Niche Specialization:**
   - **Target Audience:** Define a specific client demographic, industry, or type of work to create a tailored service offering.
   - **Unique Selling Proposition:** Develop a unique selling proposition (USP) that sets your services apart from the competition.
4. **Test and Refine:**
   - **Portfolio Building:** Offer sample work or discounted rates to build a strong portfolio and garner testimonials.

- **Pilot Projects:** Experiment with small-scale projects to assess profitability and interest before expanding.

Setting Up a Freelance Business:

Once you've identified profitable opportunities, the next step is to build a sustainable and scalable freelance business.

1. **Legal and Financial Setup:**
   - **Business Structure:** Choose a business structure (sole proprietorship, LLC, corporation) that offers the best balance of liability protection and tax benefits.
   - **Licensing and Permits:** Ensure compliance with local regulations regarding licensing or permits.
   - **Separate Finances:** Open a separate business bank account and establish a record-keeping system for taxes and expenses.
2. **Professional Branding:**
   - **Business Name:** Choose a business name that is memorable and reflects your services.
   - **Logo and Visual Identity:** Create a logo, color palette, and visual branding to distinguish your business.
   - **Website and Portfolio:** Build a professional website with an engaging portfolio showcasing your expertise and testimonials.
3. **Client Acquisition Strategies:**
   - **Freelancing Platforms:** Register on major freelancing platforms and tailor your profile to the desired client base.
   - **Networking:** Leverage social networks, industry events, and referrals to build strong relationships with potential clients.
   - **Content Marketing:** Share informative blog posts, videos, or social media updates to establish thought leadership and attract clients organically.
   - **Direct Outreach:** Email or call prospective clients with a personalized pitch detailing how your services can address their needs.

4. **Pricing and Contracts:**
    - **Pricing Models:** Offer various pricing models such as hourly rates, fixed project fees, or retainers.
    - **Contracts and Agreements:** Create comprehensive contracts that outline the scope, deliverables, payment terms, and confidentiality.
5. **Time Management and Productivity:**
    - **Routine and Scheduling:** Establish a consistent work routine, blocking time for focused project work, client communication, and skill development.
    - **Project Management Tools:** Use tools like Trello, Asana, or Monday.com to streamline project timelines and deadlines.
    - **Healthy Boundaries:** Set clear boundaries with clients regarding work hours and response times.
6. **Financial Planning and Growth:**
    - **Budgeting and Savings:** Develop a budget that accounts for variable income and expenses, and create an emergency fund to handle potential lean periods.
    - **Skill Development:** Invest in courses, workshops, and certifications to expand your skillset and improve service quality.
    - **Diversification:** Add new services or complementary offerings to reduce dependence on a single income stream.
7. **Client Retention and Feedback:**
    - **Relationship Building:** Prioritize communication and transparency to build long-term relationships with clients.
    - **Feedback and Improvement:** Regularly seek client feedback to refine your services and identify growth areas.

The freelance revolution offers significant opportunities for individuals seeking financial independence. By identifying profitable opportunities and establishing a strong business foundation, you can achieve flexible and scalable income while building a rewarding career aligned with your skills and passions.

Chapter 7: Turning Hobbies into Profits
Case Studies of Successful Hobby-Based Businesses:

1. **Photography: Jasmine Star**
   - **Background:** Jasmine Star transitioned from law school to professional photography after discovering her passion for capturing moments. Her initial success came from wedding photography, where she built a reputation for unique storytelling.
   - **Growth Strategy:** Recognizing a gap in education, she launched an online platform offering photography workshops and digital marketing strategies. Her blog and social media engagement created a strong community of aspiring photographers.
   - **Outcome:** Jasmine turned her hobby into a thriving business through wedding photography, digital courses, and speaking engagements, inspiring countless photographers along the way.

2. **Crafting: Martha Stewart**
   - **Background:** Martha Stewart started with a passion for cooking and crafting, leveraging her love of homemaking into a catering business. Recognizing the potential of lifestyle content, she began writing and sharing tips across a range of hobbies.
   - **Growth Strategy:** By publishing books and magazines and hosting a TV show, Stewart turned crafting, cooking, and gardening into a media empire. She emphasized quality and creativity, setting new standards in lifestyle content.
   - **Outcome:** Martha Stewart became synonymous with homemaking, expanding into merchandising, e-commerce, and branding, making her a household name.

3. **Fitness: Blogilates**

- **Background:** Cassey Ho, the creator of Blogilates, combined her passion for fitness and design into an influential YouTube channel focusing on pilates workouts. Her engaging, energetic style resonated with viewers worldwide.
- **Growth Strategy:** Beyond fitness videos, Cassey monetized her platform by selling fitness apparel, accessories, and exercise plans. She diversified her brand into subscription memberships and online courses.
- **Outcome:** Blogilates became one of the top fitness brands on YouTube, growing into a multi-million-dollar business.

Steps to Monetize Personal Passions:

1. **Evaluate Market Viability:**
   - **Identify Marketable Skills:** Assess your hobbies to determine which ones are marketable. What knowledge or expertise can you offer that others value?
   - **Market Research:** Investigate online platforms (Etsy, YouTube, Instagram) and communities to understand current demand, pricing, and gaps in the market.
2. **Create a Business Plan:**
   - **Define Your Audience:** Clearly identify your target demographic, understanding their preferences and buying behavior.
   - **Unique Selling Proposition:** Develop a compelling USP that differentiates your offering from competitors, whether through quality, creativity, or storytelling.
   - **Financial Model:** Calculate the costs of production, marketing, and distribution. Set achievable revenue goals to ensure profitability.
3. **Start Small and Experiment:**
   - **Prototype or Beta Test:** Launch a prototype or offer your services on a small scale to gather feedback and refine your product.

- **Minimum Viable Product (MVP):** Avoid perfectionism and focus on delivering an MVP to gauge customer interest and response.

4. **Develop Your Brand and Online Presence:**
   - **Brand Identity:** Create a cohesive brand identity that conveys your values, style, and story through logos, color schemes, and messaging.
   - **Website and Social Media:** Build a professional website that showcases your products or services. Use social media to share engaging content, build community, and attract potential customers.
   - **Content Marketing:** Create tutorials, behind-the-scenes videos, or blog posts that offer value, building credibility and loyalty.

5. **Diversify Monetization Streams:**
   - **Product Sales:** Sell handcrafted goods, digital products, or merchandise directly through your website or third-party platforms.
   - **Service-Based:** Offer consulting, coaching, workshops, or freelance services.
   - **Digital Content:** Monetize through ads, sponsored content, affiliate marketing, or memberships/subscriptions.
   - **Licensing and Collaborations:** License designs or partner with established brands for co-branded products.

6. **Networking and Community Building:**
   - **Collaborate with Influencers:** Partner with influencers or like-minded businesses for cross-promotion and expanded reach.
   - **Networking Events:** Attend trade shows, webinars, and industry events to meet potential customers and partners.
   - **Customer Engagement:** Foster a supportive community through email marketing, webinars, and exclusive offers.

7. **Scale and Optimize:**
   - **Outsource and Automate:** Delegate non-core tasks like

shipping or marketing to focus on creative work. Automate repetitive tasks to save time.

- **Data-Driven Improvements:** Analyze customer data to identify popular products or areas for improvement. Test different pricing models and refine your marketing approach.
- **Expand Offerings:** Diversify your offerings into new formats or product lines to reach wider audiences and generate more revenue.

Monetizing hobbies requires patience, persistence, and a passion-driven approach. By understanding market demands and strategically scaling your business, you can build a sustainable income source that brings fulfillment and prosperity.

Chapter 8: Investing for Beginners
Basics of Stocks, Bonds, and Mutual Funds:

1. **Stocks:**
   - **Definition:** Stocks represent ownership in a company. When you purchase shares, you become a partial owner, entitling you to a share of the company's profits and voting rights.
   - **Types of Stocks:**
       - **Common Stocks:** Most traded, offering voting rights and dividends (when declared).
       - **Preferred Stocks:** Provide fixed dividends and have higher claim priority but usually lack voting rights.
   - **Risks and Rewards:**
       - **Potential for High Returns:** Stocks generally offer higher returns than bonds over the long term due to growth potential.
       - **Volatility:** Prices fluctuate significantly based on market sentiment, company performance, and macroeconomic conditions.
2. **Bonds:**
   - **Definition:** Bonds are debt securities where an investor loans money to a corporation or government in exchange for periodic interest payments and the return of the principal at maturity.
   - **Types of Bonds:**

- **Government Bonds:** Issued by governments, typically lower risk.
- **Corporate Bonds:** Issued by companies, offering higher yields but carrying higher risk.
- **Municipal Bonds:** Issued by local governments, often offering tax benefits.
  - **Risks and Rewards:**
    - **Stable Returns:** Bonds are less volatile than stocks, providing stable returns through interest payments.
    - **Interest Rate Sensitivity:** Bond prices generally fall when interest rates rise, affecting overall value.
    - **Default Risk:** Corporate bonds are subject to the risk that the issuer may default.

3. **Mutual Funds:**
   - **Definition:** Mutual funds pool money from many investors to purchase diversified securities, managed by professional portfolio managers.
   - **Types of Mutual Funds:**
     - **Equity Funds:** Invest primarily in stocks, targeting capital appreciation.
     - **Bond Funds:** Focus on generating stable income through bonds.
     - **Balanced Funds:** Combine stocks and bonds to balance risk and return.
     - **Index Funds:** Passively managed, mimicking the performance of a market index (e.g., S&P 500).
   - **Risks and Rewards:**
     - **Diversification:** Reduces individual security risk, providing exposure to different sectors or regions.
     - **Management Fees:** Actively managed funds often carry higher fees that can eat into returns.

How to Start with a Small Investment:

1. **Define Investment Goals:**
   - **Short-Term Goals:** Emergencies, travel, or major purchases (1-3 years). Consider more conservative, low-risk investments like bonds.
   - **Medium-Term Goals:** Buying a home or saving for college (3-10 years). Balanced portfolios with moderate risk are appropriate.
   - **Long-Term Goals:** Retirement or wealth-building (10+ years). Stocks and equity-focused mutual funds suit these goals.

2. **Build a Financial Foundation:**
   - **Emergency Fund:** Set aside 3-6 months' worth of living expenses in a liquid savings account to cover unexpected emergencies.
   - **Debt Management:** Reduce high-interest debt, as the cost outweighs potential investment returns.

3. **Understand Your Risk Tolerance:**
   - **Personal Comfort Level:** Gauge your emotional response to market fluctuations and ability to absorb losses.
   - **Time Horizon:** Longer time horizons allow for higher risk tolerance, given the potential for market recovery.

4. **Choose an Investment Platform:**
   - **Brokerage Accounts:** Full-service or discount brokers offer access to various securities. Choose platforms with low fees and diverse investment options.
   - **Robo-Advisors:** Automated platforms that build and manage diversified portfolios based on your goals and risk tolerance.
   - **Employer-Sponsored Accounts:** 401(k) or 403(b) accounts often have tax benefits and employer matching.

5. **Start Investing:**
   - **Low-Cost Index Funds or ETFs:** These passive investments provide diversification with minimal fees.

- **Dividend Reinvestment Plans (DRIPs):** Automatically reinvest dividends to grow your investment over time.
- **Dollar-Cost Averaging:** Invest a fixed amount regularly to reduce the impact of market volatility.

6. **Monitor and Rebalance:**
   - **Periodic Review:** Assess your portfolio periodically to ensure it's aligned with your goals and risk tolerance.
   - **Rebalancing:** Adjust your portfolio to maintain the desired asset allocation, selling overperforming assets and buying underperforming ones.

7. **Seek Continuous Education:**
   - **Books, Podcasts, and Online Courses:** Increase your investment knowledge by reading investment books, listening to financial podcasts, or enrolling in courses.
   - **Financial Advisors:** Consider consulting a certified financial planner (CFP) for tailored advice if needed.

Starting with small investments can be the beginning of a journey toward financial independence. By understanding different investment vehicles, setting clear goals, and maintaining discipline, even modest investments can grow substantially over time, leading to sustainable prosperity.

Chapter 9: Real Estate Ventures
Understanding the Real Estate Market:

1. **Market Fundamentals:**
   - **Supply and Demand:** The basic principles of supply and demand heavily influence real estate prices. High demand with limited supply generally leads to price appreciation, while oversupply can suppress prices.
   - **Economic Indicators:** Monitor key indicators such as employment rates, GDP growth, interest rates, and consumer confidence. Economic booms often drive up property values, while downturns can have the opposite effect.
   - **Regional Trends:** Real estate markets vary significantly based on region. Urban areas often see higher prices and rental demand compared to rural markets due to job availability, amenities, and population density.

2. **Types of Real Estate:**
   - **Residential:** Properties designed for living, such as single-family homes, multi-family units, condos, and apartments. These are often easier for beginners due to their familiarity and steady rental demand.
   - **Commercial:** Properties used for business purposes like offices, retail spaces, and industrial units. They often require larger investments and come with more complex regulations.
   - **Mixed-Use:** Combine commercial and residential units, providing diverse income streams.
   - **Specialty Properties:** Include hotels, vacation rentals, healthcare facilities, or self-storage, often requiring specific expertise.

3. **Market Cycles:**
   - **Recovery:** Prices begin to stabilize or rise after a downturn.

Investors typically find good deals on undervalued properties during this phase.

- **Expansion:** Property values rise rapidly due to strong demand, and new construction picks up.
- **Hyper Supply:** New construction oversupplies the market, leading to a price plateau or decline.
- **Recession:** Oversupply causes prices to drop, often due to rising vacancy rates.

4. **Financing Options:**

- **Conventional Loans:** Traditional loans typically requiring a 20% down payment and good credit.
- **Government-Backed Loans:** FHA or VA loans offer favorable terms for qualifying individuals, including lower down payments.
- **Private Lenders:** Individuals or companies providing loans with different terms than conventional lenders, often used for investment properties.
- **Cash:** Allows investors to avoid interest and fees, potentially securing better deals.

Strategies for Rental Income and Flipping Houses:

1. **Rental Income:**

- **Long-Term Rentals:** Rent properties to tenants under long-term leases, providing steady monthly income.
  - **Tenant Screening:** Carefully vet tenants for creditworthiness, rental history, and reliability to minimize issues.
  - **Property Management:** Either self-manage or hire a property management company to handle maintenance, rent collection, and tenant communication.
  - **Cash Flow Analysis:** Ensure rent exceeds mortgage payments, property taxes, insurance, and maintenance costs to generate positive cash flow.

- **Short-Term Rentals:** List properties on vacation rental platforms like Airbnb or VRBO for short stays.
  - **High Occupancy Rates:** Target tourist-friendly locations or urban areas with consistent demand.
  - **Local Regulations:** Understand and comply with zoning laws, licensing, and taxation requirements for short-term rentals.
  - **Dynamic Pricing:** Adjust pricing based on seasonality, demand, and local events to maximize income.

2. **House Flipping:**
   - **Research and Due Diligence:**
     - **Neighborhood Selection:** Find neighborhoods with potential for appreciation or undergoing revitalization.
     - **Comparative Market Analysis:** Identify undervalued properties by comparing them to recently sold homes in the same area.
   - **Renovation Strategy:**
     - **Budgeting:** Create a renovation budget, accounting for labor, materials, permits, and contingencies.
     - **Project Management:** Coordinate contractors, permits, and timelines to minimize delays and cost overruns.
     - **Design Improvements:** Focus on high-ROI improvements like kitchens, bathrooms, and curb appeal to maximize the property's market value.
   - **Selling Strategy:**
     - **Target Audience:** Tailor renovations to the expected buyer demographic (first-time homebuyers, families, luxury market).
     - **Staging and Marketing:** Stage the home professionally and work with an experienced real estate agent for effective marketing.

- ■ **Pricing:** Set competitive pricing by comparing recently sold similar homes, ensuring room for profit.

3. **Diversification:**
   - ○ **Real Estate Investment Trusts (REITs):** Invest in publicly traded REITs for diversification without directly owning properties.
   - ○ **Crowdfunding:** Participate in real estate crowdfunding platforms that pool investor funds to buy commercial properties.

4. **Mitigating Risks:**
   - ○ **Market Research:** Continuously monitor market trends, local regulations, and economic indicators.
   - ○ **Insurance:** Carry appropriate insurance, including landlord insurance and liability coverage.
   - ○ **Emergency Fund:** Maintain a reserve fund to cover unexpected vacancies, repairs, or market downturns.

Real estate ventures offer compelling opportunities for wealth building and financial independence, whether through steady rental income or the fast-paced gains of house flipping. By understanding the market and choosing strategies that align with your risk tolerance, skills, and financial goals, you can pave the path to prosperity in real estate.

Chapter 10: E-commerce Opportunities
Starting an Online Store:

1. **Market Research and Niche Selection:**
   - **Identify Profitable Niches:** Study consumer trends and search data to identify gaps in the market or high-demand products with limited competition. Analyze competitors to determine where you can offer better value.
   - **Target Audience:** Develop detailed buyer personas based on demographic, geographic, and behavioral factors. Understand their pain points and tailor your product selection and marketing messages accordingly.
2. **Product Sourcing and Inventory Management:**
   - **Manufacturers and Wholesalers:** Build relationships directly with manufacturers or wholesalers for better margins and reliable quality.
   - **Dropshipping:** Partner with suppliers to handle inventory and shipping directly to customers. It requires no upfront inventory investment but can limit quality control.
   - **Private Labeling:** Rebrand existing products under your own label. This option combines the flexibility of sourcing with the ability to establish your brand identity.
3. **Store Setup and Platform Selection:**
   - **E-commerce Platforms:**
     - **Shopify:** Offers easy-to-use tools, templates, and third-party apps for building, customizing, and managing your store.
     - **WooCommerce:** An open-source WordPress plugin providing full control and flexibility over the store's design and functionality.
     - **BigCommerce:** Provides robust built-in features like SEO tools, multi-channel selling, and payment integrations.

- **Custom Website:** For unique design and branding, work with a developer to build a custom e-commerce website.
- **Store Design and User Experience:**
    - **Intuitive Navigation:** Organize products by categories and enable search functions to help users find what they need quickly.
    - **Mobile Optimization:** Ensure your store is mobile-friendly since most shoppers use mobile devices.
    - **Checkout Experience:** Provide multiple payment methods, minimize required form fields, and offer a guest checkout option.

4. **Marketing and Customer Acquisition:**
    - **Search Engine Optimization (SEO):** Optimize product pages, blog posts, and meta descriptions for relevant keywords to drive organic traffic.
    - **Content Marketing:** Create engaging blog posts, how-to guides, videos, or social media posts that resonate with your audience, establishing authority and trust.
    - **Social Media Advertising:** Leverage Facebook, Instagram, and Pinterest to target specific audiences with appealing visuals and compelling calls to action.
    - **Influencer Partnerships:** Collaborate with influencers whose followers align with your target market for authentic promotion.

5. **Customer Retention and Service:**
    - **Email Marketing:** Build an email list through pop-up offers, and send regular newsletters, exclusive deals, or personalized recommendations.
    - **Loyalty Programs:** Reward repeat purchases with points, discounts, or special privileges to encourage long-term customer loyalty.
    - **Customer Support:** Provide responsive customer support via chat, email, or phone. Address queries and complaints promptly to improve satisfaction.

6. **Analytics and Optimization:**
   - **Key Performance Indicators (KPIs):** Monitor metrics like customer acquisition cost, conversion rates, average order value, and customer lifetime value.
   - **A/B Testing:** Experiment with different headlines, images, and layouts to determine the most effective design elements.
   - **Continuous Improvement:** Regularly update your store based on data insights, customer feedback, and evolving market trends.

Leveraging Platforms like Amazon and eBay:

1. **Amazon Selling:**
   - **Seller Types:** Choose between "Individual" (pay per item sold) or "Professional" (monthly subscription) accounts based on your sales volume.
   - **Fulfillment by Amazon (FBA):** Ship inventory to Amazon warehouses. They handle storage, packaging, and shipping to customers, offering fast shipping with Prime eligibility.
   - **Product Listings:**
     - **SEO Optimization:** Use relevant keywords and high-quality images to make your products stand out.
     - **Product Descriptions:** Write concise, persuasive descriptions that highlight key features and benefits.
   - **Amazon Advertising:** Use sponsored product ads or headline search ads to boost visibility and drive traffic.
2. **eBay Selling:**
   - **Listing Types:** Choose between "Auction" (for unique items) or "Fixed Price" (Buy It Now) listings. Consider store subscriptions for higher volume sales.
   - **Categories and Keywords:** List products in the appropriate categories and include relevant keywords for better search visibility.
   - **Global Shipping Program:** Reach international buyers

easily through eBay's shipping program, handling customs forms and delivery.

- **Best Offer Feature:** Attract more buyers by allowing them to negotiate a lower price, increasing the chances of a sale.

3. **General Strategies for Success:**

- **Repricing Tools:** Automate pricing adjustments to stay competitive without manual intervention.
- **Cross-Promotion:** Bundle complementary items or suggest related products to increase order value.
- **Customer Feedback:** Encourage reviews and promptly address any negative feedback to maintain high ratings.

Scaling and Diversification:

1. **Marketplaces Expansion:** List on other platforms like Etsy (for handmade items), Walmart Marketplace, or niche-specific sites to diversify your revenue streams.
2. **Private Label Expansion:** Identify high-performing products and develop your private label brand to increase margins and differentiate your store.
3. **Multi-Channel Fulfillment:** Sync inventory across your website, Amazon, and other channels using integrated inventory management software.
4. **Global Reach:** Investigate international markets for potential demand and customize offerings to cater to local preferences and regulations.

E-commerce presents vast opportunities for entrepreneurs seeking financial freedom. By thoroughly understanding your audience, optimizing your store, and leveraging the power of established marketplaces, you can build a sustainable and scalable online business, opening up thousands of paths to prosperity.

Chapter 11: Digital Products and Automation
Creating and Selling Digital Goods (e-Books, Courses, Software):

1. **Understanding Digital Goods:**
   - **Benefits:** They can be reproduced and distributed without additional production costs, leading to higher profit margins. Distribution is global, allowing access to a wider audience.
   - **Types of Digital Products:**
     - **e-Books:** Guides, fiction, non-fiction, or specialized knowledge texts that provide value in specific niches.
     - **Online Courses:** Video, audio, and written educational material packaged to teach specific skills or knowledge.
     - **Software:** Apps, plugins, and tools that solve particular user problems or enhance productivity.
2. **Creating Digital Products:**
   - **Identify Market Needs:**
     - **Niche Research:** Study current market trends and identify gaps that your product could fill.
     - **Target Audience:** Create detailed buyer personas to guide content creation and ensure your product meets their needs.
   - **Content Creation:**
     - **e-Books:** Plan, write, and format your e-book with clear chapters, engaging content, and attractive visuals. Use platforms like Canva for design or outsource to a professional designer.
     - **Courses:** Structure your course with logical progression, starting from foundational to advanced lessons.

Use varied formats like video lectures, quizzes, and assignments to enhance engagement.

- **Software Development:** Identify core features, create wireframes or prototypes, and code using agile methods. Consider user testing for valuable feedback.

3. **Selling Platforms and Distribution:**
   - **Self-Publishing Platforms:** Amazon Kindle Direct Publishing (KDP) and Apple Books offer global reach for self-published e-books.
   - **Learning Management Systems (LMS):** Platforms like Teachable, Udemy, and Thinkific help host and market your courses while managing enrollment and payments.
   - **Standalone Website:**
     - **e-Commerce Integration:** Integrate payment gateways and digital product management for smooth transactions.
     - **Marketing Automation:** Use email marketing and social media automation to build your brand.
   - **Software Marketplaces:** Distribute software on marketplaces like the Apple App Store, Google Play, or Code-Canyon.

4. **Marketing and Scaling:**
   - **Content Marketing:** Share relevant blog posts, videos, or podcasts that highlight your expertise and the value of your digital product.
   - **Lead Magnets:** Offer free sample chapters, mini-courses, or trial versions to attract potential customers.
   - **Affiliate Marketing:** Partner with influencers or other businesses to expand your reach, offering them commissions for each sale they generate.

Using Automation to Maximize Profits:

1. **Sales Funnels and Customer Journeys:**

- **Lead Generation:**
  - **Landing Pages:** Create optimized landing pages focused on specific audiences or products.
  - **Webinars:** Host automated webinars that engage potential customers and introduce your digital products.
- **Email Automation:** Segment leads based on interests or behavior and send targeted content through autoresponder sequences to nurture relationships and increase conversions.

2. **Customer Support:**
   - **Chatbots:** Automate customer inquiries with AI chatbots that can handle FAQs, provide product recommendations, and escalate issues to human agents when necessary.
   - **Help Centers:** Create a self-serve knowledge base or FAQ section with comprehensive guides and tutorials.

3. **Analytics and Data-Driven Optimization:**
   - **Customer Segmentation:** Use customer data to personalize marketing messages, product recommendations, and promotions.
   - **A/B Testing:** Continuously test landing pages, email content, and ad creatives to refine what resonates most with different segments.

4. **Upselling and Cross-Selling:**
   - **Product Bundles:** Package complementary products together or offer them as add-ons at checkout to increase the average order value.
   - **Follow-Up Sequences:** Send follow-up emails recommending related products after a purchase.

5. **Recurring Revenue Models:**
   - **Subscription Services:** Offer access to exclusive content, premium courses, or software features for a monthly or annual fee.
   - **Membership Sites:** Provide ongoing access to new content, community forums, or expert consultations through a membership model.

6. **Continuous Improvement:**
    - **Customer Feedback:** Regularly survey customers and analyze reviews to identify areas of improvement for your digital products.
    - **Market Trends:** Stay updated with evolving industry trends to refine your offerings and keep them relevant.

Creating and automating the sale of digital products opens vast opportunities for passive income. By understanding the needs of your audience and using effective automation strategies, you can streamline your business, scale profits, and work towards true financial freedom in less than 30 days.

Chapter 12: Passive Income Streams
Introduction to Passive Income:

1. **Definition and Benefits:**
   - **What is Passive Income?** Revenue generated with minimal ongoing effort after an initial setup or investment. Examples include rental properties, royalties, and automated businesses.
   - **Benefits:**
     - **Financial Freedom:** Provides financial stability through diversified, steady cash flows.
     - **Flexibility:** Once established, it requires minimal time, giving you freedom to explore new ventures.
     - **Scalability:** Many passive income streams can be scaled up to increase revenue without a proportional increase in effort.
2. **Active vs. Passive:**
   - **Active Income:** Requires consistent effort, such as traditional employment or service-based businesses.
   - **Passive Income:** Involves upfront work or investment, with income flowing over time with little additional work.
3. **Misconceptions:**
   - **No Effort Myth:** Passive income requires significant effort initially. While maintenance is minimal, it still requires monitoring.
   - **Immediate Returns:** Building passive income streams takes time, planning, and patience before yielding consistent returns.

Ideas for Generating Ongoing Revenue:

1. **Investments:**

- ◦ **Dividend Stocks:** Invest in companies that pay regular dividends to shareholders. Consider companies with a history of consistent dividend payouts.
- ◦ **Bonds and Fixed-Income Securities:** Government or corporate bonds that pay periodic interest. Municipal bonds offer tax advantages, while high-yield bonds provide higher returns with added risk.
- ◦ **Real Estate Investment Trusts (REITs):** Publicly traded companies that own or finance income-generating real estate and distribute at least 90% of taxable income as dividends.

2. **Real Estate:**
   - ◦ **Rental Properties:** Acquire residential or commercial properties and rent them out for monthly income.
     - ■ **Property Management:** Either manage the property yourself or hire a professional property manager to handle tenants, maintenance, and rent collection.
   - ◦ **Short-Term Rentals:** Utilize vacation rental platforms like Airbnb or VRBO to earn more per night than traditional rentals.
   - ◦ **Real Estate Crowdfunding:** Pool investments with others to fund property projects, receiving a share of the profits or interest income.

3. **Digital Products:**
   - ◦ **e-Books:** Write and publish e-books in high-demand niches and sell them through platforms like Amazon KDP or Apple Books.
   - ◦ **Online Courses:** Develop comprehensive courses and sell them on platforms like Udemy or your own website.
   - ◦ **Software and Apps:** Build apps or software that solve a specific problem, offering them on subscription or one-time purchase models.

4. **Licensing and Royalties:**
   - ◦ **Creative Works:** Earn royalties on creative works like books,

music, photography, and videos. Platforms like Shutterstock and YouTube offer creators revenue-sharing models.
- **Franchising:** License your successful business model to franchisees who pay initial fees and a percentage of ongoing revenue.

5. **Automated Businesses:**
   - **Drop Shipping:** Create an e-commerce store where suppliers fulfill and ship orders directly to customers.
   - **Affiliate Marketing:** Promote products or services on your website, blog, or social media channels, earning commissions on resulting sales.
   - **Ad Revenue:** Run ads on a high-traffic website, blog, or YouTube channel to earn ongoing advertising income.

6. **Intellectual Property Monetization:**
   - **Patents:** License patents to companies for manufacturing or usage rights in exchange for royalties.
   - **Trademarks:** License trademarks to other businesses that want to use your brand for their products.

7. **Financial Products:**
   - **Peer-to-Peer Lending:** Lend money on P2P platforms, receiving interest payments over time.
   - **Annuities:** Purchase annuity contracts from insurance companies, which provide a fixed income stream after a specified period.

8. **Subscription Services:**
   - **Membership Sites:** Provide exclusive content or services to members who pay a recurring fee.
   - **Subscription Boxes:** Curate themed boxes of products and deliver them to subscribers monthly.

Maximizing Passive Income:

1. **Diversify Streams:** Invest in multiple passive income sources to mitigate risks and maximize returns.

2. **Reinvest Earnings:** Reinvest profits into existing or new income streams to build compound growth.
3. **Monitor and Adjust:** Regularly review the performance of each stream and make necessary adjustments to improve profitability.
4. **Leverage Technology:** Automate repetitive tasks like email marketing, payment collection, and customer support using technology.

By understanding the principles and identifying the right opportunities, you can create a resilient portfolio of passive income streams that work tirelessly for your financial freedom, bringing you closer to becoming financially free in 30 days.

Chapter 13: Tax Strategies for Maximizing Wealth
Legal Ways to Reduce Tax Liabilities:

1. **Tax Deductions:**
   - **Business Expenses:** Deduct ordinary and necessary expenses related to running a business, like office supplies, travel, and marketing. Home-based businesses can also deduct a portion of home office expenses.
   - **Charitable Donations:** Donations to qualifying charities are deductible up to 60% of your adjusted gross income (AGI).
   - **Medical Expenses:** Deduct out-of-pocket medical and dental expenses exceeding 7.5% of AGI.
   - **Educational Expenses:** Tax credits like the Lifetime Learning Credit or the American Opportunity Tax Credit help offset tuition costs.
   - **Mortgage Interest:** Deduct interest paid on mortgages up to a certain limit. This can be a significant deduction for homeowners.
2. **Tax Credits:**
   - **Earned Income Tax Credit (EITC):** A credit for low- to moderate-income workers and families, potentially reducing the amount of tax owed.
   - **Child and Dependent Care Credit:** Covers a portion of child or dependent care expenses while you work or look for work.
   - **Retirement Savings Contributions Credit:** A non-refundable credit for contributions made to eligible retirement accounts.
3. **Retirement Accounts:**
   - **Traditional IRAs and 401(k)s:** Contributions to these

accounts are tax-deductible, reducing taxable income in the current year. Earnings grow tax-deferred until retirement.

- **Roth IRAs:** Contributions are made with post-tax income, but qualified withdrawals are tax-free.
- **Self-Employed Retirement Plans:** Plans like SEP IRAs, SIMPLE IRAs, and Solo 401(k)s allow self-employed individuals to contribute more to retirement accounts and reduce taxable income.

4. **Income Splitting and Family Tax Strategies:**
   - **Hiring Family Members:** Hire family members in your business and pay them reasonable wages. Their earnings might be taxed at a lower rate if they're in a lower tax bracket.
   - **Education Accounts:** Set up tax-advantaged accounts like 529 plans to save for children's education while reducing estate tax implications.
   - **Family Gifts:** Gift up to $16,000 annually (as of 2024) per recipient without incurring gift tax.

5. **State and Local Tax Strategies:**
   - **State Tax Credits:** Research local tax incentives for things like renewable energy installations, education, or historic building renovations.
   - **Tax-Friendly States:** Consider relocating or structuring businesses in states with no income tax or favorable corporate tax structures.

6. **Legal Entity Selection:**
   - **S-Corporation:** Profits pass through to shareholders and are taxed at individual rates, while avoiding double taxation.
   - **Limited Liability Company (LLC):** Offers the flexibility to choose pass-through taxation or corporate taxation, depending on business needs.

Tax Benefits for Various Investments:

1. **Real Estate:**
   - **Depreciation Deductions:** Deduct the annual depreciation of rental property to reduce taxable income.
   - **1031 Exchange:** Defer capital gains taxes by reinvesting proceeds from the sale of a property into a similar investment.
   - **Opportunity Zones:** Invest in designated economically distressed areas to receive significant tax benefits, including deferral or exclusion of gains.
2. **Stock Market Investments:**
   - **Long-Term Capital Gains:** Pay reduced tax rates on investments held for over a year.
   - **Tax-Loss Harvesting:** Offset gains by selling underperforming assets to realize losses, reducing overall tax liability.
   - **Qualified Dividends:** Certain dividends are taxed at long-term capital gains rates.
3. **Retirement and Education Accounts:**
   - **529 Plans:** Contributions grow tax-free, and qualified withdrawals for education expenses are not taxed.
   - **Health Savings Accounts (HSAs):** Contributions are tax-deductible, and distributions for qualified medical expenses are tax-free.
   - **401(k) Loans:** Borrow against your 401(k) without triggering a taxable event.
4. **Business Investments:**
   - **Qualified Small Business Stock (QSBS):** Gains from the sale of QSBS (held for at least five years) may be excluded from federal taxes up to a certain limit.
   - **Research and Development Credits:** Offset the costs of innovation and product development.
5. **Green and Renewable Investments:**
   - **Renewable Energy Credits:** Receive tax credits for investing in solar, wind, or other renewable energy projects.
   - **Energy-Efficient Property:** Certain energy-efficient improvements qualify for federal tax credits.

Developing a Comprehensive Tax Strategy:

1. **Work with Professionals:** Engage tax professionals like CPAs or tax attorneys who understand complex tax laws and can devise a tailored strategy.
2. **Stay Informed:** Tax laws change frequently, so staying current with tax reforms is vital to ensure compliance and leverage new opportunities.
3. **Document Everything:** Keep detailed records of deductions and credits to substantiate claims in case of an audit.
4. **Proactive Planning:** Review and adjust your tax strategy regularly, especially after significant life events or business changes.

Implementing legal tax strategies can dramatically reduce your tax burden, allowing you to retain more income and reinvest in your path to financial freedom.

Chapter 14: Advanced Investment Strategies Techniques for Forex and Crypto Trading:

1. **Forex Trading Strategies:**
   - **Fundamental Analysis:**
     - **Economic Indicators:** Analyze key data like GDP growth, unemployment rates, and inflation. These indicators shape monetary policy, impacting currency values.
     - **Central Bank Policies:** Understand how interest rates, quantitative easing, and other monetary measures influence exchange rates.
     - **Geopolitical Factors:** Political instability or elections can significantly impact forex markets, so it's crucial to monitor global events.
   - **Technical Analysis:**
     - **Chart Patterns:** Recognize trends and patterns like head and shoulders, triangles, and double tops/bottoms.
     - **Indicators and Oscillators:** Use moving averages, RSI (Relative Strength Index), and MACD (Moving Average Convergence Divergence) to gauge market momentum and potential reversals.
     - **Support and Resistance Levels:** Identify crucial price levels where currencies tend to reverse or consolidate, informing entry and exit points.
   - **Trading Approaches:**
     - **Day Trading:** Capitalize on intraday price movements by holding positions for a few minutes or hours, usually exiting by market close.
     - **Swing Trading:** Hold positions for several days to

capture medium-term trends, blending technical and fundamental analysis.

- **Position Trading:** Maintain long-term positions based on macroeconomic trends and long-term charts, ranging from weeks to months.

○ **Risk Management:**

- **Stop-Loss Orders:** Limit losses by exiting a position when it reaches a predetermined price.

- **Position Sizing:** Base trade sizes on risk tolerance, balancing potential rewards against the risk of each position.

- **Leverage Caution:** Use leverage carefully, understanding that it can amplify gains but also losses.

2. **Cryptocurrency Trading Strategies:**

○ **Understanding Blockchain Technology:**

- **Basics:** Grasp how decentralized networks, consensus mechanisms, and cryptographic security underpin cryptocurrencies.

- **Use Cases:** Identify real-world applications for different tokens, such as decentralized finance (DeFi) and NFTs.

○ **Market Analysis:**

- **Technical Analysis:** Apply chart patterns, candlestick formations, and technical indicators similar to forex trading.

- **On-Chain Analysis:** Monitor blockchain data, such as transaction volume, wallet balances, and network activity, to assess investor behavior.

- **Sentiment Analysis:** Analyze social media, forums, and news to gauge market sentiment and predict potential trends.

○ **Investment Approaches:**

- **HODL (Hold on for Dear Life):** Purchase promising

cryptocurrencies and hold for extended periods to ride out volatility.

- **Day Trading:** Profit from price swings within a day using technical analysis and fast execution.
- **Staking and Yield Farming:** Earn passive income by staking tokens or participating in DeFi protocols to earn interest or governance tokens.

◦ **Risk Management:**
- **Portfolio Diversification:** Spread investments across multiple cryptocurrencies and fiat currencies to hedge against extreme volatility.
- **Cold Storage:** Secure significant holdings in offline wallets to minimize hacking risks.
- **Regulatory Awareness:** Stay updated on government regulations regarding exchanges, taxation, and trading to avoid compliance issues.

Diversifying Investment Portfolios:

1. **Principles of Diversification:**
   ◦ **Reducing Risk:** Diversification reduces the impact of any single investment's poor performance on your overall portfolio.
   ◦ **Uncorrelated Assets:** Invest in assets that don't move in sync with each other to balance gains and losses.
2. **Asset Classes:**
   ◦ **Equities:** Invest in stocks, either through individual shares or mutual funds/ETFs, to participate in corporate growth and dividend income.
   ◦ **Bonds:** Fixed-income securities offer predictable returns and reduce overall portfolio volatility, especially in economic downturns.
   ◦ **Commodities:** Hedge against inflation and market down-

turns by investing in gold, silver, oil, and agricultural products.

- **Real Estate:** Property investments offer stable cash flows through rentals and long-term appreciation potential.
- **Alternative Investments:** Venture into private equity, hedge funds, collectibles, or art for higher returns with greater risks.
- **Cryptocurrencies:** Gain exposure to this rapidly evolving sector with high return potential but extreme volatility.

3. **Portfolio Strategies:**
- **Strategic Asset Allocation:**
  - **Risk Tolerance:** Determine acceptable risk levels based on your financial goals, time horizon, and investment knowledge.
  - **Target Allocation:** Allocate specific percentages to each asset class, periodically rebalancing to maintain these ratios.
- **Tactical Asset Allocation:** Adjust asset allocations dynamically in response to market trends and economic outlooks.
- **Core-Satellite Approach:** Maintain a stable core portfolio of index funds, with smaller satellite investments in high-risk/high-reward opportunities.

4. **Geographical Diversification:**
- **Domestic and International Markets:** Invest in global equities, bonds, and real estate to hedge against country-specific risks.
- **Emerging Markets:** Diversify into emerging economies to capture higher growth rates despite increased political and currency risks.

5. **Sectoral Diversification:**
- **Different Sectors:** Avoid overexposure to any one industry by investing in multiple sectors like technology, healthcare, finance, and consumer goods.

6. **Monitoring and Rebalancing:**

- ◦ **Regular Reviews:** Periodically review portfolio performance and macroeconomic trends to make adjustments.
- ◦ **Rebalancing:** Rebalance investments periodically or when market movements cause significant changes to the target asset allocation.

By understanding the intricacies of advanced trading techniques and adopting a diversified portfolio approach, you can maximize potential returns while effectively managing risks. Mastering these strategies will solidify your financial freedom journey and help you become financially free in 30 days.

Chapter 15: Leveraging Business Credit
How to Build and Use Business Credit:

1. **Understanding Business Credit:**
   - **Definition:** Business credit refers to a business's ability to borrow money based on its financial health and credit-worthiness. It's separate from the personal credit of the business owner.
   - **Purpose:** Establishing a solid business credit profile can help secure funding for expansion, improve cash flow, and negotiate favorable terms with suppliers.
2. **Establishing a Business Credit Profile:**
   - **Incorporate Your Business:**
     - **Legal Entity:** Form a corporation or an LLC to separate business finances from personal assets.
     - **Tax Identification Number:** Obtain an EIN (Employer Identification Number) from the IRS for tax purposes.
   - **Business Bank Accounts:**
     - **Dedicated Accounts:** Open a separate bank account to manage business transactions and establish a financial identity distinct from personal accounts.
     - **Merchant Accounts:** Accept credit card payments to improve cash flow and demonstrate revenue consistency.
   - **Business Address and Phone Number:**
     - **Separate Address:** Avoid using your home address as the business location to appear more credible to lenders.
     - **Dedicated Phone Line:** Obtain a separate business phone number listed in business directories.
3. **Securing Vendor and Supplier Credit:**
   - **Trade Lines:** Establish accounts with suppliers that offer

net-30 or net-60 terms, meaning you pay within 30 or 60 days.

- **Vendor Reporting:** Ensure these vendors report payment history to business credit reporting agencies like Dun & Bradstreet, Experian, and Equifax.

4. **Building a Positive Credit History:**
   - **Business Credit Cards:**
     - **Dedicated Cards:** Use cards specifically for business expenses and pay them off regularly to demonstrate repayment ability.
     - **Credit Utilization:** Keep credit utilization below 30% of the credit limit to avoid appearing over-leveraged.
   - **Line of Credit:**
     - **Secured or Unsecured:** Apply for a business line of credit to cover short-term funding needs while building credit history.
   - **Loans and Leases:**
     - **Small Business Loans:** Take out manageable loans from local banks, credit unions, or the Small Business Administration (SBA) to establish repayment records.
     - **Equipment Leasing:** Lease equipment instead of purchasing outright, creating another tradeline on your credit report.

5. **Monitoring and Improving Business Credit Scores:**
   - **Credit Reports:**
     - **Regular Monitoring:** Periodically review reports from all major business credit bureaus to check for errors or discrepancies.
     - **Dispute Inaccuracies:** Report and resolve incorrect information promptly to maintain a clean record.
   - **Payment Timeliness:** Pay all obligations on time or early to build a reputation for reliability.

6. **Maintaining Financial Stability:**

- **Profitability:** Maintain profitability and positive cash flow to reflect financial strength.
- **Financial Statements:** Provide up-to-date and accurate financial statements when applying for credit or negotiating terms.

Advantages of Credit for Entrepreneurs:

1. **Funding Business Expansion:**
   - **Capital for Growth:** Secure credit to fund new locations, marketing campaigns, or inventory increases without tapping personal finances.
   - **Leverage:** Use credit to capitalize on business opportunities and scale operations efficiently.
2. **Improved Cash Flow:**
   - **Working Capital:** Cover daily operating expenses during slower sales periods or while waiting for customer payments.
   - **Seasonal Businesses:** Address seasonal fluctuations by stocking up on inventory or increasing staff with short-term credit.
3. **Establishing Credibility:**
   - **Vendor Trust:** Develop strong relationships with suppliers who may offer better pricing or favorable terms once trust is established.
   - **Investor Confidence:** Demonstrate fiscal responsibility to attract potential investors or partners.
4. **Protection of Personal Finances:**
   - **Limited Liability:** Keep personal assets separate from business liabilities in the event of business debt defaults.
   - **Credit Protection:** Avoid relying on personal credit for business purposes, protecting your personal credit score.
5. **Access to Higher Credit Limits:**
   - **Larger Loans:** Strong business credit opens doors to higher loan amounts for expansion or refinancing debt.

- ○ **Negotiating Power:** Better credit scores provide leverage to negotiate lower interest rates and favorable repayment terms.

6. **Emergency Preparedness:**
   - ○ **Unexpected Expenses:** Maintain a business line of credit or emergency fund to handle unexpected costs like equipment failure or sudden market downturns.
   - ○ **Business Continuity:** Access to emergency funds allows you to sustain operations during crises.

7. **Investment Opportunities:**
   - ○ **New Ventures:** Utilize credit to diversify your business or enter new markets with minimal initial cash outlay.
   - ○ **Asset Acquisition:** Acquire assets that generate passive income, like rental properties or intellectual property, using business credit.

In summary, developing and leveraging business credit can significantly enhance your ability to grow, sustain, and diversify your business while providing the financial flexibility necessary for long-term success and prosperity.

Chapter 16: Franchising and Business Opportunities
Evaluating Franchise Opportunities:

1. **Understanding the Franchise Business Model:**
   - **Definition and Concept:** A franchise is a licensed business model where a franchisor grants rights to a franchisee to operate under their brand, using established systems and processes.
   - **Key Components:**
     - **Franchise Agreement:** Legally binding contract outlining the rights, obligations, and expectations of both franchisor and franchisee.
     - **Franchise Fee and Royalties:** Initial and ongoing payments for brand usage, support, and training.
2. **Assessing Personal Alignment and Readiness:**
   - **Interest and Passion:** Ensure alignment between personal interests and the franchise's industry or product.
   - **Skills and Experience:** Evaluate personal and managerial skills relevant to running the chosen franchise successfully.
3. **Financial Evaluation:**
   - **Total Costs:**
     - **Initial Investment:** Franchise fees, training expenses, equipment, real estate, and working capital requirements.
     - **Ongoing Costs:** Monthly royalties, marketing fees, and operational expenses.
   - **Profitability Projections:**
     - **Revenue Potential:** Analyze projected revenue based on market demand, location, and existing franchisees' performance.

- **Break-Even Analysis:** Determine how long it will take to break even and start generating a profit.
  - **Access to Capital:** Ensure access to funding through personal savings, loans, or investor partnerships.

4. **Market Research:**
   - **Franchise Industry Trends:**
     - **Growth Sectors:** Identify sectors experiencing significant growth, such as fitness, food and beverage, or education.
     - **Consumer Behavior:** Analyze consumer trends that may impact specific franchise industries.
   - **Competition Analysis:**
     - **Direct and Indirect Competitors:** Assess the competitive landscape for existing brands and substitute products.
     - **Market Saturation:** Avoid oversaturated markets where competition could hinder growth.

5. **Franchisor Evaluation:**
   - **Brand Strength:**
     - **Recognition and Reputation:** Evaluate brand awareness and customer loyalty.
     - **Franchise Performance:** Assess the success rate of existing franchisees.
   - **Support Systems:**
     - **Training:** Verify the extent of initial and ongoing training, from product knowledge to business management.
     - **Marketing:** Understand the franchisor's marketing strategy and support, including national campaigns, social media, and local marketing.
   - **Franchise Disclosure Document (FDD):**
     - **Litigation History:** Check for previous or ongoing lawsuits involving the franchisor.

- **Financial Health:** Review audited financial statements to ensure the franchisor's fiscal stability.

6. **Legal and Regulatory Considerations:**
   - **Franchise Regulations:** Understand regional and national regulations governing franchise operations.
   - **Legal Review:** Seek legal advice to ensure clarity and fairness in the franchise agreement.

Steps to Acquire and Manage a Franchise:

1. **Initial Contact and Inquiry:**
   - **Research:** Identify promising franchises that align with your goals and values.
   - **Contact Franchisors:** Reach out to franchisors for more detailed information about their business model, support systems, and costs.

2. **Application Process:**
   - **Application Submission:** Submit an application to demonstrate interest and basic qualifications.
   - **Discovery Day:** Attend franchisor-hosted events or tours to gain firsthand insights into the brand and meet key personnel.

3. **Franchise Agreement Negotiation:**
   - **Legal Review:** Work with a franchise attorney to understand the franchise agreement and negotiate terms, such as territorial exclusivity or initial fees.
   - **Finalization:** Sign the agreement once satisfied with the terms and conditions.

4. **Business Plan Development:**
   - **Operations Plan:** Outline day-to-day management, staffing, and customer service strategies.
   - **Marketing Strategy:** Develop a comprehensive plan to promote the franchise locally, leveraging national marketing support where applicable.

- **Financial Projections:** Create realistic revenue projections, budgets, and timelines for growth.

5. **Securing Funding:**
   - **Loan Applications:** Apply for financing through banks, SBA programs, or private investors.
   - **Personal Savings or Partners:** Utilize personal savings or seek partnerships to cover initial and working capital costs.

6. **Location Selection and Setup:**
   - **Site Selection:** Choose a high-traffic location that aligns with the franchisor's demographic requirements and customer base.
   - **Renovation and Equipment:** Renovate the site as per brand guidelines and install necessary equipment.

7. **Training and Staffing:**
   - **Initial Training:** Attend franchisor-led training sessions to understand brand standards, products, and management.
   - **Hiring:** Recruit and train staff to deliver consistent customer experiences.

8. **Opening and Marketing:**
   - **Soft Opening:** Conduct a pre-launch event to fine-tune operations.
   - **Grand Opening:** Hold a grand opening with promotional offers to attract initial customers.
   - **Local Marketing:** Utilize local media, social media, and events to build brand awareness.

9. **Ongoing Management and Growth:**
   - **Daily Operations:** Monitor operations, ensuring compliance with brand standards and maximizing customer satisfaction.
   - **Franchisor Communication:** Maintain regular communication with the franchisor to stay updated on best practices, new products, or promotions.
   - **Expansion:** Consider opening additional franchise units once the first is successful.

Acquiring and managing a franchise requires a thorough evaluation of opportunities and the diligent application of effective management practices. By navigating this process strategically, aspiring entrepreneurs can unlock a lucrative path to financial freedom.

Chapter 17: Making Money with Social Media
Strategies for Monetizing Social Media Platforms:

1. **Affiliate Marketing:**
   - **Definition:** Promote products or services of other companies through unique affiliate links, earning a commission for each sale.
   - **Choosing Affiliate Programs:**
     - **Relevance:** Select programs related to your niche to align with audience interests and ensure higher conversion rates.
     - **Commission Rates:** Compare payout structures across programs, balancing upfront rates with recurring commissions.
     - **Trustworthiness:** Partner with reputable companies to maintain audience trust.
   - **Promotional Techniques:**
     - **Content Integration:** Seamlessly integrate affiliate links into blog posts, videos, and reviews, providing valuable context.
     - **Coupons and Deals:** Share exclusive offers or discounts with your audience to encourage sales.
2. **Sponsored Content and Brand Partnerships:**
   - **Influencer Marketing:**
     - **Sponsored Posts:** Create content showcasing a brand's product or service for a fee, adhering to disclosure guidelines.
     - **Brand Ambassadorships:** Form long-term relationships where you consistently represent and promote the brand.
   - **Negotiating Deals:**

- **Content Strategy:** Define deliverables, frequency, and style of posts to ensure clear expectations.
  - **Compensation:** Determine fair rates based on your follower count, engagement, and industry norms.
- **Maintaining Authenticity:**
  - **Relevance:** Promote only products that align with your brand values and audience needs to retain credibility.
  - **Transparency:** Clearly disclose sponsorships to adhere to advertising regulations and maintain trust.

3. **Selling Digital Products and Services:**
   - **Courses and E-books:**
     - **Educational Content:** Develop and sell online courses or e-books that address your audience's pain points or learning goals.
     - **Membership Sites:** Offer exclusive content to members who pay monthly or annual fees for access.
   - **Consulting and Coaching:**
     - **Expertise:** Provide one-on-one coaching, group sessions, or personalized consulting based on your industry expertise.
     - **Client Acquisition:** Use social media to build a reputation and attract potential clients through testimonials, free resources, and case studies.

4. **YouTube Monetization:**
   - **YouTube Partner Program:**
     - **Eligibility:** Meet the criteria of 1,000 subscribers and 4,000 watch hours in the past 12 months to qualify.
     - **Ad Revenue:** Earn from display, overlay, and video ads placed on your videos based on impressions and clicks.
   - **Alternative Income Streams:**
     - **Channel Memberships:** Provide perks to viewers

who pay a monthly membership fee, such as exclusive badges or live chat access.
- **Super Chats:** Enable viewers to purchase highlighted messages during live streams to engage directly.
- **Sponsorships and Merchandising:**
    - **Product Placement:** Partner with brands for product placements within your videos.
    - **Merchandising:** Sell branded merchandise like clothing, mugs, or accessories through integrated store links.

5. **Livestreaming and Donations:**
   - **Platforms:** Use Twitch, YouTube Live, Facebook Live, or TikTok Live to engage audiences in real-time.
   - **Donation Features:**
       - **Bits and Cheers:** Twitch's virtual currency allows viewers to tip streamers during broadcasts.
       - **Virtual Gifts:** Viewers on TikTok Live can send virtual gifts, which can be converted into cash.
   - **Subscription Models:** Offer premium subscription plans for exclusive content, behind-the-scenes access, or personalized shoutouts.

Building a Personal Brand Online:

1. **Identifying Your Niche:**
   - **Passion and Expertise:** Focus on topics that align with your passion and expertise to remain consistent and authentic.
   - **Market Research:** Analyze competitors, trends, and audience interests to find gaps or unique angles in your chosen niche.

2. **Crafting Your Unique Value Proposition:**
   - **Purpose and Mission:** Develop a mission statement that conveys your brand's purpose and values.

- ◦ **Target Audience:** Define the demographics, interests, and pain points of your ideal followers.

3. **Content Strategy:**
   - ◦ **Content Pillars:** Identify 3-5 core topics or themes that form the foundation of your brand's messaging.
   - ◦ **Posting Schedule:** Maintain a consistent posting frequency tailored to each platform's algorithms.
   - ◦ **Content Formats:** Mix long-form posts, videos, stories, reels, and polls to appeal to different audience segments.

4. **Visual Identity:**
   - ◦ **Logo and Color Palette:** Create a logo and consistent color scheme to build instant brand recognition.
   - ◦ **Templates and Fonts:** Use templates and fonts across posts, banners, and profile pictures for cohesive branding.

5. **Engagement and Community Building:**
   - ◦ **Interaction:**
     - ■ **Comments and Messages:** Respond promptly to comments and direct messages to foster connection and loyalty.
     - ■ **Live Sessions:** Host live Q&As or webinars to answer questions and interact directly with your audience.
   - ◦ **User-Generated Content:** Encourage followers to share testimonials, reviews, or creative content featuring your brand, offering recognition or incentives in return.

6. **Analytics and Refinement:**
   - ◦ **Performance Metrics:**
     - ■ **Engagement:** Track likes, shares, comments, and views to gauge the effectiveness of your content.
     - ■ **Growth Rate:** Monitor follower count and website traffic to measure the impact of your brand-building efforts.
   - ◦ **Refinement:** Continuously refine your strategy based on feedback, trends, and performance data to align with evolving audience interests.

Monetizing social media and building a strong personal brand can be highly profitable with a well-structured strategy. By leveraging various platforms and content formats while consistently engaging your audience, you can create a sustainable path to financial freedom.

Chapter 18: Unusual Investments and Collectibles
Investing in Art, Antiques, and Collectibles:

1. **Understanding Unconventional Investments:**
   - **Definition:** Unconventional investments include non-traditional assets like art, antiques, rare coins, wine, and collectibles that generally don't fit into mainstream investment categories like stocks or real estate.
   - **Purpose:** They offer diversification for investors seeking alternatives to traditional financial instruments and can serve as a hedge against inflation.
2. **Categories of Unconventional Investments:**
   - **Art:**
     - **Paintings and Sculptures:** Include works from established and emerging artists across various styles and movements.
     - **Photography and Digital Art:** Growing fields with contemporary appeal and increasing market demand.
   - **Antiques:**
     - **Furniture and Decorative Arts:** High-quality pieces from specific eras or regions hold historical and aesthetic value.
     - **Jewelry and Timepieces:** Unique or vintage jewelry and watches can appreciate due to their rarity and craftsmanship.
   - **Collectibles:**
     - **Coins and Stamps:** Rare coins and stamps often command high prices due to historical significance and limited supply.
     - **Wine and Spirits:** Collectible wine and spirits can increase in value due to their age and scarcity.
     - **Memorabilia and Toys:** Sports memorabilia, trading

cards, and vintage toys have passionate collectors and strong resale markets.

3. **Identifying High-Potential Assets:**
   - **Market Trends and Demand:**
     - **Research:** Study auction results, gallery exhibits, and collector forums to identify trends and emerging interests.
     - **Artist or Maker Reputation:** Evaluate the significance of an artist or craftsman in their field and potential future demand.
   - **Rarity and Provenance:**
     - **Limited Supply:** Scarcity drives value, especially for unique items like original artworks or rare vintages.
     - **Provenance:** Trace the ownership history and authenticity to establish an asset's credibility and origin.
   - **Condition:**
     - **Restoration and Preservation:** Assess the condition and restoration history of art or antiques, which significantly affects value.

4. **Buying and Selling Unconventional Investments:**
   - **Acquisition Channels:**
     - **Auctions:** Purchase through public or private auctions for access to rare and high-quality pieces.
     - **Dealers and Galleries:** Work with reputable dealers and galleries to ensure quality and authenticity.
     - **Direct Sales:** Engage in direct sales with collectors or estates to negotiate favorable prices.
   - **Selling Strategies:**
     - **Auction Consignment:** Consign pieces to auctions with strong interest in the specific category for higher visibility.
     - **Private Sales:** Arrange private sales through dealer networks or collector groups for more control over pricing.

- Timing:
  - **Market Timing:** Monitor economic conditions and demand cycles to determine the best time to sell.

5. **Valuation and Pricing:**
   - **Appraisals:** Obtain professional appraisals from certified experts to gauge the fair market value of an asset.
   - **Comparables:** Compare recent sales of similar items to estimate current market value.
   - **Sentiment:** Consider market sentiment and investor interest in specific categories, which can impact valuations.

Risks and Rewards of Unconventional Investments:

1. **Potential Rewards:**
   - **Diversification:**
     - **Uncorrelated Returns:** These investments often perform independently of traditional markets, providing diversification.
   - **Cultural Value:** They can offer intrinsic cultural and aesthetic value in addition to financial returns.
   - **Hedging Against Inflation:** Physical assets, like art or antiques, can retain value during inflationary periods.
   - **Rising Demand:** Growing interest in certain collectibles or art movements can drive significant appreciation over time.

2. **Risks to Consider:**
   - **Liquidity:**
     - **Low Liquidity:** Selling unconventional assets may require specialized markets, leading to longer holding periods.
   - **Valuation Challenges:**
     - **Subjectivity:** Determining value can be subjective, relying heavily on expert opinions and comparable sales.

- **Volatility:** Market trends can shift quickly, affecting demand and pricing unpredictably.
- **Fraud and Forgeries:**
  - **Authenticity Concerns:** Forgeries or misrepresented provenance can lead to substantial financial losses.
  - **Due Diligence:** Investing in reputable dealers and requiring certificates of authenticity are essential.
- **Storage and Maintenance:**
  - **Environmental Risks:** Proper storage and climate control are crucial to prevent deterioration or damage.
  - **Insurance Costs:** High-value pieces require specialized insurance, increasing overall holding costs.

3. **Investment Strategies:**
- **Portfolio Balance:**
  - **Asset Allocation:** Consider unconventional investments as part of a balanced portfolio, limiting exposure to avoid over-reliance.
- **Niche Expertise:**
  - **Education:** Develop deep knowledge in specific categories or consult experts to guide acquisition and management.
  - **Networking:** Build relationships with collectors, curators, and dealers to gain insights and access to exclusive opportunities.
- **Long-Term Perspective:**
  - **Patient Capital:** Expect holding periods to be longer, focusing on the gradual appreciation of assets rather than quick returns.

Unconventional investments, while riskier than traditional investments, can bring significant rewards and value to a diversified portfolio when approached strategically and with thorough due diligence.

Chapter 19: Financial Freedom through Minimalism
How Simplifying Your Life Can Save Money:

1. **Concept of Minimalism:**
   - **Definition:** Minimalism is a lifestyle philosophy focused on reducing clutter and distractions to prioritize meaningful experiences, relationships, and financial security.
   - **Key Principles:**
     - **Intentional Living:** Deliberate choices about consumption and time usage to align with core values.
     - **Decluttering:** Eliminating non-essential possessions that do not contribute to happiness or purpose.
2. **Financial Benefits of Minimalism:**
   - **Reduced Consumption:**
     - **Spending Habits:** With fewer possessions to maintain or replace, minimalists spend less on consumer goods and luxury items.
     - **Impulse Buying:** By being more intentional, impulse buying and emotional shopping are minimized, leading to savings.
   - **Lower Debt:**
     - **Credit Card Use:** Focusing on essentials often means less reliance on credit cards and a reduction in revolving debt.
     - **Auto Loans:** By choosing to own fewer or smaller vehicles, or using public transportation, auto-related debt can be minimized.
   - **Smaller Housing Costs:**
     - **Downsizing:** Living in a smaller home reduces mortgage payments, property taxes, utilities, and maintenance expenses.

- **Renting:** Renting instead of owning can lower costs related to repairs and insurance.
- **Sustainable Consumption:**
    - **Quality Over Quantity:** Investing in higher-quality, durable goods reduces the need for frequent replacements.
    - **DIY Skills:** Learning to repair or repurpose items extends their life and reduces spending on replacements.

3. **Practical Strategies for Simplifying:**
    - **Decluttering and Organizing:**
        - **Methodical Purging:** Gradually eliminate non-essential possessions by category or room, focusing on items unused in the past year.
        - **Donation or Resale:** Donate usable items to charity or resell them online to generate extra income.
    - **Intentional Purchasing:**
        - **30-Day Rule:** Wait 30 days before buying non-essential items to ensure they align with your values and budget.
        - **Capsule Wardrobe:** Build a versatile wardrobe with high-quality staples that can be mixed and matched.
    - **Mindful Consumption:**
        - **Subscriptions:** Regularly review and cancel unused streaming services, gym memberships, or subscriptions.
        - **Food Planning:** Plan weekly meals and limit dining out to reduce grocery costs and food waste.

4. **Time Management and Prioritization:**
    - **Simplify Schedules:**
        - **Non-Essential Activities:** Reduce commitments and social obligations that do not align with personal goals or values.
        - **Work-Life Balance:** Emphasize quality over quantity

in professional life to reduce burnout and regain personal time.

- ○ **Prioritize Relationships:**
    - ■ **Family and Friends:** Focus on deepening meaningful relationships with close family and friends instead of maintaining many casual acquaintances.
    - ■ **Solo Time:** Create time for self-care, hobbies, or creative pursuits that enrich your personal growth.

Case Studies of Individuals Who Have Thrived through Minimalism:

1. **Emma's Story - Downsizing to Financial Security:**
    - ○ **Background:** Emma worked a high-stress corporate job and owned a large home with a hefty mortgage.
    - ○ **Minimalism Journey:**
        - ■ **Downsizing:** She sold her home and moved to a small apartment, saving on mortgage, utilities, and maintenance.
        - ■ **Career Shift:** Transitioned to freelance work, freeing her schedule and allowing her to pursue creative hobbies.
        - ■ **Financial Impact:** With drastically reduced expenses, Emma now saves over 40% of her income and has established a solid emergency fund.
2. **Ryan's Story - Simplified Wardrobe and Lifestyle:**
    - ○ **Background:** Ryan struggled with debt after spending on designer clothes and high-end gadgets to fit in with social circles.
    - ○ **Minimalism Journey:**
        - ■ **Decluttering:** Sold most of his expensive clothing and gadgets, sticking to a capsule wardrobe and basic gadgets.

- **Intentional Budget:** Created a strict budget to curb unnecessary spending and prioritize essentials.
- **Financial Impact:** Paid off credit card debt within a year and now allocates significant savings toward investments and travel.

3. **Laura's Story - Sustainable Living through Minimalism:**
    - **Background:** Laura was concerned about her ecological footprint and overspending on disposable products.
    - **Minimalism Journey:**
        - **Zero Waste:** She adopted a zero-waste lifestyle, eliminating disposable plastics and packaging.
        - **DIY Projects:** Learned to repair and repurpose items instead of buying new.
        - **Financial Impact:** Reduced monthly expenses by 30% and built a sustainable emergency fund with the savings.

4. **Michael's Story - Prioritizing Freedom and Experiences:**
    - **Background:** Michael realized that long work hours left him exhausted and unable to enjoy life fully.
    - **Minimalism Journey:**
        - **Career Realignment:** Switched to a part-time job that paid less but offered more flexibility and creative fulfillment.
        - **Travel Focus:** Opted to spend more on travel and experiences than material possessions.
        - **Financial Impact:** His expenses decreased significantly, and he uses savings to fund trips while maintaining an emergency fund.

Minimalism, when practiced thoughtfully, empowers individuals to reclaim their finances, time, and mental space, enabling them to pursue financial freedom and live intentionally. By focusing on what truly matters, people can thrive with fewer possessions, lower expenses, and more meaningful experiences.

Chapter 20: Travel Hacking
Techniques for Cheap Travel and Living Abroad:

1. **Introduction to Travel Hacking:**
   - **Definition:** Travel hacking is the art of strategically leveraging airline miles, credit card points, and other travel rewards to travel more affordably.
   - **Purpose:** The goal is to maximize travel experiences by reducing the overall cost of flights, accommodations, and other expenses.
2. **Mastering Rewards Programs:**
   - **Credit Card Rewards:**
     - **Sign-Up Bonuses:** Apply for travel rewards credit cards offering large sign-up bonuses and meet the minimum spend to earn the bonus points.
     - **Strategic Spending:** Use travel cards for everyday expenses to accumulate points quickly, especially in bonus categories like dining, groceries, or gas.
     - **Redeeming Points:** Understand redemption rates and transfer partners to maximize value when exchanging points for flights or hotels.
   - **Airline Miles:**
     - **Frequent Flyer Programs:** Join multiple frequent flyer programs to take advantage of their specific perks and partner airlines.
     - **Earning Miles:** Earn miles through flights, credit card transfers, or partner promotions like dining or shopping programs.
     - **Award Flights:** Use miles for award flights, prioritiz-

ing off-peak travel dates and flexible itineraries for the best availability and rates.

- **Hotel Loyalty Programs:**
    - **Membership Benefits:** Join loyalty programs of major hotel chains to access exclusive member discounts, free nights, and upgrades.
    - **Status Matching:** Some hotel chains offer status matching with other loyalty programs, providing elite perks across chains.

3. **Budget Travel Techniques:**
    - **Low-Cost Carriers:**
        - **Budget Airlines:** Opt for budget airlines or low-cost carriers for short-haul or regional flights, being mindful of additional fees.
        - **Booking Timing:** Book flights during flash sales or well in advance to secure the lowest fares.
    - **Alternative Accommodations:**
        - **Hostels:** Stay at hostels for affordable rates and a social atmosphere, often providing free or low-cost amenities like breakfast and Wi-Fi.
        - **Home Rentals:** Platforms like Airbnb and Vrbo offer private rooms or whole homes at lower costs than hotels, especially for long-term stays.
        - **House Sitting:** Exchange house sitting services for free accommodation through platforms like TrustedHousesitters or MindMyHouse.
    - **Transportation Savings:**
        - **Public Transport:** Use local public transportation instead of taxis or rental cars for significant savings.
        - **Passes:** Purchase city or regional transportation passes for unlimited travel within a given time frame.

4. **Living Abroad on a Budget:**
    - **Expat-Friendly Countries:**
        - **Low Cost of Living:** Countries with favorable

exchange rates and lower living costs can offer a high quality of life for less money.

- **Visa Policies:** Research visa policies and long-term stay options for retirees, digital nomads, or entrepreneurs.

◦ **Local Adaptation:**

- **Language Learning:** Basic language skills can help reduce costs by avoiding tourist pricing and accessing local markets.

- **Cultural Awareness:** Understanding cultural norms and negotiation practices helps in renting accommodation and purchasing goods.

Using Travel to Create New Business Opportunities:

1. **Travel Blogging and Vlogging:**
   ◦ **Content Creation:**

   - **Blog Posts and Videos:** Share travel tips, destination guides, or personal experiences through blogs or YouTube channels.

   - **Affiliate Marketing:** Earn commissions by promoting travel gear, credit cards, or tour packages through affiliate links.

   - **Sponsored Content:** Partner with travel brands or tourism boards to create sponsored content in exchange for fees or free trips.

   ◦ **Monetization:**

   - **Ad Revenue:** Generate passive income through ads displayed on your blog or YouTube channel.

   - **Products and Services:** Offer e-books, guides, or consulting services based on your travel expertise.

2. **Remote Freelancing:**
   ◦ **Digital Nomad Lifestyle:**

   - **Freelance Skills:** Leverage skills in writing, web

design, marketing, or programming to work remotely while traveling.

- **Clients:** Build a client base that allows for flexible schedules and the ability to work from anywhere with internet access.

- **Co-Working Spaces:**
  - **Networking Opportunities:** Use co-working spaces to network with other freelancers or entrepreneurs for collaborations.
  - **Facilities:** Access reliable internet, printing, and meeting facilities while traveling.

3. **Import/Export Business:**
   - **Sourcing Unique Goods:**
     - **Local Artisans:** Find unique handicrafts, textiles, or specialty products that can be exported to other markets.
     - **Wholesale Suppliers:** Establish relationships with reliable suppliers for consistent quality and pricing.
   - **Market Research:**
     - **Demand:** Identify markets where these products have a significant demand and low competition.
     - **Regulations:** Understand import/export regulations, taxes, and logistics to streamline the process.

4. **Tourism and Hospitality Ventures:**
   - **Tours and Activities:**
     - **Customized Tours:** Create personalized or niche tour packages catering to specific interests like adventure, history, or gastronomy.
     - **Guided Activities:** Lead specialized activities like diving trips, wine tasting, or cultural excursions.
   - **Accommodation Services:**
     - **Hostels and Guesthouses:** Operate small-scale hostels or guesthouses for budget travelers seeking a local experience.

- **Vacation Rentals:** Invest in properties to rent out on vacation rental platforms.

By mastering travel hacking techniques and exploring creative ways to monetize travel experiences, it's possible to significantly reduce costs and create new income streams, leading to greater financial freedom while satisfying the desire to explore the world.

Chapter 21: Building a Business Empire
Strategies for Scaling Small Businesses:

1. **The Fundamentals of Scaling:**
   - **Vision and Strategy:**
     - **Clear Vision:** Develop a clear, inspiring vision that guides growth and aligns the team with business objectives.
     - **Strategic Planning:** Craft a strategic plan for expansion that includes market analysis, financial forecasting, and realistic goals.
   - **Market Positioning:**
     - **Unique Value Proposition:** Refine your unique value proposition to distinguish your brand in competitive markets.
     - **Customer Segmentation:** Understand key customer segments and tailor marketing to meet their needs.
2. **Infrastructure and Systems:**
   - **Operational Efficiency:**
     - **Standard Operating Procedures:** Establish and document standard operating procedures (SOPs) to streamline workflows and ensure quality.
     - **Automation:** Leverage automation software to manage inventory, billing, customer support, and other repetitive tasks.
   - **Supply Chain Management:**
     - **Suppliers and Logistics:** Build strong relationships with suppliers to ensure reliable sourcing and efficient logistics.
     - **Inventory Optimization:** Implement inventory management techniques like just-in-time to reduce holding costs and wastage.
3. **Human Resources and Leadership:**

- ○ **Team Building:**
  - ■ **Talent Acquisition:** Attract and retain talent aligned with your culture, offering career development opportunities.
  - ■ **Training and Development:** Invest in training programs to enhance employee skills and align them with growth goals.
- ○ **Delegation:**
  - ■ **Leadership Structure:** Establish a management structure that empowers leaders to make decisions and manage their departments effectively.
  - ■ **Succession Planning:** Identify potential successors and create a pipeline for future leadership to ensure continuity.

4. **Revenue Streams and Diversification:**
   - ○ **Product Diversification:**
     - ■ **New Markets:** Expand existing product lines to new geographic markets with tailored marketing and pricing strategies.
     - ■ **Complementary Products:** Develop or acquire complementary products to offer customers more comprehensive solutions.
   - ○ **Subscription Models:**
     - ■ **Recurring Revenue:** Implement subscription models that offer steady, predictable revenue streams through memberships or maintenance services.

5. **Financial Planning and Funding:**
   - ○ **Cash Flow Management:**
     - ■ **Operating Capital:** Monitor cash flow carefully to maintain sufficient working capital during periods of rapid growth.
     - ■ **Debt Management:** Use debt strategically for expansion without compromising long-term financial stability.

- Funding Options:
    - **Equity Financing:** Consider venture capital or private equity funding for large-scale expansions, while being mindful of dilution.
    - **Grants and Incentives:** Identify government grants, subsidies, or incentives that could help fund specific projects.

6. **Marketing and Brand Building:**
    - **Digital Marketing:**
        - **Content Strategy:** Develop a strong content marketing strategy to engage customers across blogs, social media, and email newsletters.
        - **SEO and SEM:** Use search engine optimization (SEO) and search engine marketing (SEM) to increase website visibility and conversions.
    - **Brand Loyalty:**
        - **Customer Engagement:** Foster a sense of community and loyalty among customers through personalized communication and loyalty programs.
        - **Brand Consistency:** Maintain consistent branding across all marketing channels to strengthen brand recognition and trust.

7. **Technology Integration:**
    - **Business Analytics:**
        - **KPIs and Dashboards:** Track key performance indicators (KPIs) and build data dashboards to inform strategic decision-making.
        - **Predictive Analytics:** Utilize predictive analytics for demand forecasting, customer behavior analysis, and trend identification.
    - **Customer Relationship Management (CRM):**
        - **Personalization:** Implement CRM systems to provide personalized marketing and sales interactions based on customer data.

Case Studies of Successful Entrepreneurs:

1. **Melinda's Story - From Local Store to Global E-Commerce:**
   - **Background:** Melinda ran a local boutique selling handmade jewelry and crafts, which initially catered to tourists in her city.
   - **Scaling Journey:**
     - **Online Expansion:** She launched an online store to reach a global audience, investing in SEO and social media ads to drive traffic.
     - **Product Line Expansion:** Developed new product lines like custom designs and DIY kits to attract new customer segments.
     - **Logistics Network:** Partnered with fulfillment centers to streamline international shipping.
   - **Outcome:** Her boutique became a thriving e-commerce business, quadrupling annual revenue in five years while maintaining a loyal customer base.
2. **Carlos's Story - From Food Truck to Franchise Chain:**
   - **Background:** Carlos started with a single food truck selling gourmet tacos, which quickly gained a local following.
   - **Scaling Journey:**
     - **Brick-and-Mortar Transition:** He opened his first brick-and-mortar location, focusing on a high-traffic area with consistent clientele.
     - **Franchising Model:** Developed a franchising model, offering franchisees training, marketing support, and a standardized menu.
     - **Brand Consistency:** Maintained consistency in branding and product quality across locations through SOPs and regular inspections.
   - **Outcome:** Carlos's business grew into a multi-state franchise chain with hundreds of locations and millions in annual revenue.

3. **Natasha's Story - Scaling a SaaS Business Globally:**
   - **Background:** Natasha founded a software-as-a-service (SaaS) company providing HR management solutions to small businesses.
   - **Scaling Journey:**
     - **International Markets:** Identified demand in emerging markets and localized the software to cater to different languages and regulations.
     - **Sales Network:** Built a sales network of regional partners to offer support and training in key markets.
     - **R&D Investment:** Invested heavily in research and development to continually innovate and stay ahead of competitors.
   - **Outcome:** Natasha's company now serves thousands of businesses worldwide and remains an industry leader in HR software.

Scaling a business requires a blend of strategic vision, operational efficiency, and market adaptability. By studying successful entrepreneurs and following proven strategies, small businesses can build resilient structures to grow into thriving empires that stand the test of time.

Chapter 22: Retirement Planning
Early Retirement Strategies:

1. **The Philosophy of Early Retirement:**
   - **Definition and Motivation:**
     - **Early Retirement:** Choosing to retire before the traditional retirement age, often in the 40s or 50s, to gain greater control over one's time.
     - **Motivations:** Common motivations include the desire for financial independence, pursuing personal passions, or spending more time with family.
   - **FIRE Movement:**
     - **Concept:** Financial Independence, Retire Early (FIRE) is a popular movement advocating aggressive saving and investing strategies to achieve early retirement.
     - **Variations:** Different variations exist, from Lean FIRE (minimalist living) to Fat FIRE (higher discretionary spending).
2. **Aggressive Saving and Frugality:**
   - **Savings Rate:**
     - **High Savings Goal:** Aim to save and invest 50% or more of your income to accelerate wealth accumulation.
     - **Budget Optimization:** Reduce discretionary spending by minimizing entertainment costs, dining out, and non-essential purchases.
   - **Frugality Mindset:**

- **Mindful Spending:** Practice mindful spending by prioritizing value and necessity over convenience or impulse buys.
- **DIY Solutions:** Learn skills like cooking, home maintenance, and repairs to avoid outsourcing basic tasks.

3. **Income Diversification and Passive Income:**
   - **Side Businesses:**
     - **Freelancing:** Start freelancing or consulting in your field to create an additional income stream.
     - **Digital Products:** Create digital products like online courses, e-books, or apps that generate passive income over time.
   - **Real Estate Income:**
     - **Rental Properties:** Invest in rental properties to earn a steady income through long-term leases or vacation rentals.
     - **REITs:** Real Estate Investment Trusts (REITs) offer a more liquid alternative to direct property ownership while providing regular dividends.

4. **Low-Cost Investing:**
   - **Index Funds:**
     - **Market Diversification:** Invest in low-cost index funds that track major market indices to diversify risk and reduce management fees.
     - **Long-Term Growth:** Hold investments over the long term to maximize compounding growth and minimize trading costs.
   - **Tax-Efficient Accounts:**
     - **Tax-Deferred Accounts:** Contribute to tax-advantaged retirement accounts (401(k), IRA) to reduce taxable income and maximize growth.

Maximizing Retirement Accounts:

1. **Understanding Retirement Account Types:**
   - **Employer-Sponsored Plans:**
     - **401(k):** An employer-sponsored plan allowing employees to contribute pre-tax income, often with an employer matching contribution.
     - **403(b):** Similar to a 401(k) but designed for non-profit and educational employees.
   - **Individual Retirement Accounts (IRAs):**
     - **Traditional IRA:** Allows individuals to contribute pre-tax income with taxes deferred until withdrawal.
     - **Roth IRA:** Contributions are made with after-tax income, but withdrawals are tax-free if certain conditions are met.

2. **Contribution Strategies:**
   - **Employer-Sponsored Plans:**
     - **Maximize Employer Match:** Contribute at least up to the maximum employer match to capture all available free money.
     - **Contribution Limits:** Understand and meet annual contribution limits to take full advantage of tax benefits.
   - **IRAs:**
     - **Eligibility and Limits:** Verify income eligibility for Roth contributions and adhere to the annual contribution limit for both Traditional and Roth IRAs.
     - **Catch-Up Contributions:** Individuals aged 50 and above can contribute additional catch-up contributions to boost retirement savings.

3. **Investment Allocation:**
   - **Risk Tolerance and Time Horizon:**
     - **Growth vs. Stability:** Younger investors can allocate more heavily to stocks for higher growth, while older investors should prioritize bonds for stability.
     - **Target-Date Funds:** Consider target-date funds that

automatically adjust allocations over time based on the investor's retirement date.

- **Portfolio Diversification:**
  - **Domestic vs. International:** Balance investments between domestic and international stocks to diversify exposure across global markets.
  - **Alternative Investments:** Include REITs or commodities for further diversification.

4. **Withdrawal Strategies:**
   - **Required Minimum Distributions (RMDs):**
     - **RMD Rules:** Understand the rules for required minimum distributions, starting at age 73 for most retirement accounts.
     - **Penalty Avoidance:** Plan withdrawals carefully to avoid penalties for under- or over-withdrawing.
   - **Tax-Efficient Withdrawals:**
     - **Tax Rate Planning:** Monitor annual income to minimize moving into higher tax brackets when withdrawing from tax-deferred accounts.
     - **Withdrawal Order:** Consider withdrawing from Roth IRAs first to reduce the tax impact on traditional IRAs or 401(k) withdrawals.

Case Studies in Retirement Planning:

1. **Samantha's Strategy - Planning for Early Retirement:**
   - **Profile:** Samantha started her career in marketing and aimed to retire by age 45.
   - **Plan Execution:**
     - **High Savings Rate:** She maintained a savings rate of over 60% through frugal living and aggressive contributions to her 401(k) and IRA.
     - **Rental Income:** Invested in rental properties,

eventually acquiring five income-generating homes over a decade.

- **Retirement Timeline:** She reached her target goal at age 43 and transitioned to managing her rental properties full-time.

2. **Tom's Strategy - Maximizing Retirement Accounts:**
   - **Profile:** Tom, a software engineer, wanted to retire at age 65 but with significant wealth.
   - **Plan Execution:**
     - **Employer Contributions:** Contributed the maximum amount annually to his 401(k), taking full advantage of employer matching.
     - **Investment Mix:** Invested in a mix of index funds, bonds, and REITs to create a diversified portfolio.
     - **Roth IRA:** Contributed to a Roth IRA for tax-free growth and minimized taxable withdrawals in retirement.

Effective retirement planning requires proactive strategies that align with your goals and current financial situation. By understanding account types, maximizing contributions, and following efficient withdrawal strategies, you can build a secure financial future that allows you to enjoy retirement, whether it arrives early or at the traditional age.

Chapter 23: Wealth Preservation
Protecting Your Assets:

1. **Risk Management and Insurance:**
   - **Identifying Risks:**
     - **Personal Risks:** Assess personal risks, such as health issues, accidents, or legal liabilities, that could threaten personal wealth.
     - **Market Risks:** Monitor economic conditions that may impact investment portfolios, including market volatility, inflation, and currency fluctuations.
     - **Property Risks:** Protect real estate investments against natural disasters, vandalism, and tenant-related issues.
   - **Insurance Solutions:**
     - **Health and Disability Insurance:** Secure comprehensive health insurance and disability coverage to mitigate the impact of major medical expenses or income loss.
     - **Property Insurance:** Purchase homeowners or renters insurance for real estate, and consider umbrella insurance to cover potential legal liabilities.
     - **Life Insurance:** Consider term or whole life insurance to protect family members or business partners in the event of death.
   - **Business Insurance:**
     - **Liability Coverage:** Business owners should have general liability insurance and industry-specific coverage, like malpractice or errors and omissions insurance.
     - **Key Person Insurance:** Protect the business from potential financial losses due to the death or incapacity of key personnel.

2. **Diversification:**
   - **Investment Diversification:**
     - **Asset Classes:** Spread investments across different asset classes (stocks, bonds, real estate, commodities) to minimize the impact of any single market downturn.
     - **Geographic Diversification:** Reduce regional risk by investing in both domestic and international markets.
   - **Income Diversification:**
     - **Multiple Streams:** Develop multiple income streams, including dividends, rental income, and royalties, to maintain cash flow even if one source dries up.

3. **Fraud Protection and Financial Monitoring:**
   - **Digital Security:**
     - **Cybersecurity Measures:** Use strong passwords, multi-factor authentication, and reputable security software to protect financial information.
     - **Phishing Awareness:** Stay vigilant against phishing scams that can compromise online banking credentials or personal data.
   - **Credit Monitoring:**
     - **Credit Reports:** Regularly review credit reports for inaccuracies or unauthorized activity.
     - **Freeze Credit:** Consider freezing credit with major bureaus to prevent identity theft or fraudulent credit applications.

Legal Structures for Holding Wealth:

1. **Trusts and Estate Planning:**
   - **Revocable vs. Irrevocable Trusts:**
     - **Revocable Trusts:** Allow the grantor to retain control over assets and make changes as needed, offering flexibility in estate planning.
     - **Irrevocable Trusts:** Transfer control of assets to a

trustee, providing creditor protection and estate tax benefits but limiting future modifications.

- **Types of Trusts:**
  - **Living Trusts:** Protect assets during the grantor's lifetime and simplify the transfer process upon death, avoiding probate.
  - **Charitable Trusts:** Enable donors to contribute to a charitable cause while reducing their taxable estate.
  - **Special Needs Trusts:** Provide financial support for beneficiaries with disabilities without affecting their eligibility for government benefits.

2. **Limited Liability Companies (LLCs):**
   - **Asset Protection:**
     - **Separate Entity:** An LLC separates business assets from personal assets, limiting liability exposure in the event of a business lawsuit or debt.
     - **Real Estate Holdings:** Use LLCs to hold rental properties, shielding personal finances from tenant-related liabilities or property issues.
   - **Tax Advantages:**
     - **Pass-Through Taxation:** LLCs generally offer pass-through taxation, where income is taxed only once at the individual level.

3. **Family Limited Partnerships (FLPs):**
   - **Wealth Transfer:**
     - **Family Control:** FLPs allow family members to transfer ownership interests while retaining control over the partnership's assets and operations.
     - **Gifting Opportunities:** FLPs provide a means to gift partnership interests to family members while reducing estate tax implications.
   - **Creditor Protection:**
     - **Limited Partner Status:** Family members receive

protection against creditors since they have limited partner status, limiting their personal liability.

4. **Offshore Trusts and International Entities:**
   - **Offshore Trusts:**
     - **Jurisdictional Benefits:** Offshore trusts located in stable jurisdictions can offer enhanced asset protection and privacy benefits.
     - **Tax Implications:** Understand the complex tax and reporting requirements to ensure compliance with domestic and international regulations.
   - **International Business Companies (IBCs):**
     - **Global Operations:** IBCs facilitate international operations and investments, especially for individuals or businesses with cross-border interests.
     - **Financial Privacy:** Certain jurisdictions offer more privacy around ownership and transaction details, though increasing global regulations aim to prevent abuse.

Conclusion: Effective wealth preservation requires a multi-faceted approach that includes risk management, diversification, and legally sound structures. By utilizing insurance, trusts, LLCs, and other tools, individuals and businesses can minimize exposure to risks while maximizing the security of their financial legacy for future generations.

Chapter 24: Legacy Planning and Charitable Giving
Estate Planning Essentials:

1. **Importance of Estate Planning:**
   - **Defining Estate Planning:** Estate planning is the process of arranging the management and disposal of a person's estate during their life and after death.
   - **Objectives of Estate Planning:** The primary goals are to ensure assets are distributed according to one's wishes, minimize estate taxes, and prevent family disputes.
   - **Common Misconceptions:** People often think estate planning is only for the wealthy, but it benefits individuals of all financial standings.
2. **Essential Estate Planning Documents:**
   - **Last Will and Testament:**
     - **Function:** The will dictates the distribution of assets and appoints guardians for minors.
     - **Key Considerations:** Select an executor carefully, as this person will manage estate distribution and handle any legal challenges.
   - **Living Will and Healthcare Proxy:**
     - **Living Will:** Specifies one's healthcare preferences in

case of incapacity, ensuring wishes are respected regarding life-sustaining treatment.

- **Healthcare Proxy:** Appoints someone to make medical decisions on one's behalf if they become unable to do so.
- **Durable Power of Attorney:**
  - **Financial Authority:** Grants someone authority to manage one's financial matters, ensuring bills are paid and investments are managed during incapacity.

3. **Trusts as an Estate Planning Tool:**
   - **Benefits of Trusts:**
     - **Avoiding Probate:** Trusts bypass the probate process, reducing costs and delays in asset distribution.
     - **Asset Protection:** Certain trusts can shield assets from creditors and legal claims.
     - **Privacy:** Trusts offer greater confidentiality compared to wills, which become public record during probate.
   - **Types of Trusts:**
     - **Revocable Living Trust:** Allows the grantor to maintain control over assets during their lifetime and easily adjust terms.
     - **Irrevocable Trust:** Removes assets from the grantor's taxable estate but cannot be changed after creation.
     - **Charitable Trust:** Allows donors to contribute to charitable causes while receiving tax benefits and supporting beneficiaries.

4. **Minimizing Taxes and Maximizing Inheritance:**
   - **Gifting Strategies:**
     - **Annual Gift Tax Exclusion:** Gift up to the annual exclusion limit per recipient without incurring gift taxes.
     - **Lifetime Gift Tax Exemption:** Utilize the lifetime exemption to gift larger amounts while reducing the taxable estate.

- ◦ **Retirement Accounts:**
  - ■ **Beneficiary Designation:** Name beneficiaries for retirement accounts directly to transfer them outside of probate.
  - ■ **Required Minimum Distributions:** Plan withdrawals carefully to avoid excess taxes and ensure beneficiaries receive optimal distributions.

How and Why to Incorporate Philanthropy into Your Financial Plan:

1. **The Benefits of Charitable Giving:**
   - ◦ **Personal Fulfillment:**
     - ■ **Philanthropic Values:** Supporting meaningful causes enhances personal fulfillment and aligns with core values.
     - ■ **Family Engagement:** Involving family members in giving decisions can reinforce a legacy of generosity across generations.
   - ◦ **Tax Advantages:**
     - ■ **Charitable Contributions Deduction:** Itemized deductions can reduce taxable income based on the value of eligible charitable contributions.
     - ■ **Avoiding Capital Gains Taxes:** Donating appreciated securities or real estate avoids capital gains tax on the increase in value.
2. **Methods of Charitable Giving:**
   - ◦ **Direct Donations:**
     - ■ **Cash Gifts:** Cash donations are the simplest form of giving, providing immediate support to charitable organizations.
     - ■ **Donating Assets:** Donors can also contribute appreciated assets like stocks, mutual funds, or real estate.
   - ◦ **Donor-Advised Funds:**

- **Flexible Giving:** Contribute to a donor-advised fund to receive an immediate tax deduction while distributing funds over time.
- **Fund Management:** Fund managers handle administration, enabling donors to focus on selecting recipient organizations.
  - **Charitable Trusts:**
    - **Charitable Remainder Trust:** Provides income to beneficiaries for a set period, with the remainder going to a charity.
    - **Charitable Lead Trust:** Donates income to a charity first, leaving the remainder for beneficiaries after the trust term.

3. **Establishing a Legacy Foundation:**
   - **Private Family Foundations:**
     - **Mission-Focused:** Create a private family foundation to support specific causes, allowing for a lasting philanthropic legacy.
     - **Governance and Management:** Maintain full control over grantmaking and investment strategies while adhering to IRS regulations.
   - **Community Foundations:**
     - **Collaborative Giving:** Community foundations pool resources from multiple donors to support local initiatives.
     - **Simplified Administration:** Allow donors to establish funds without managing administrative tasks directly.

4. **Involving the Next Generation:**
   - **Family Meetings and Education:**
     - **Shared Values:** Host family meetings to discuss values and goals around charitable giving.
     - **Philanthropy Education:** Teach younger family

    members about philanthropy through involvement in giving decisions and volunteering.
- **Succession Planning:**
  - **Governance:** Establish clear guidelines for leadership succession and foundation governance to maintain consistency in giving priorities.
  - **Mentorship:** Senior family members can mentor the next generation, sharing insights and experiences to ensure smooth transitions.

Conclusion: Legacy planning and charitable giving are crucial components of a comprehensive financial plan. By organizing your estate carefully and integrating philanthropic values, you can ensure a secure future for your loved ones while supporting the causes that matter to you most. Protecting assets, minimizing taxes, and engaging the next generation are key steps toward leaving a meaningful legacy.

Chapter 25: Handling Financial Crises
Strategies to Manage Financial Downturns:

1. **Assessing the Situation:**
   - **Comprehensive Financial Review:**
     - **Current Financial State:** Analyze all sources of income, monthly expenses, debt obligations, and available liquid assets.
     - **Cash Flow Analysis:** Determine immediate and future cash flow requirements by distinguishing between essential and non-essential expenses.
   - **Risk Evaluation:**
     - **Market Volatility:** Assess how market changes have impacted investment portfolios and retirement savings.
     - **Job Stability:** Identify potential job vulnerabilities or upcoming layoffs that could affect regular income streams.
2. **Immediate Action Steps:**
   - **Emergency Budget:**
     - **Essential Spending:** Prioritize critical expenses like housing, utilities, and food while delaying non-essential costs like dining out or entertainment.
     - **Debt Repayment Strategy:** Focus on maintaining minimum payments to avoid penalties while prioritizing high-interest debt for extra payments if possible.
   - **Increasing Liquid Savings:**
     - **Selling Unnecessary Assets:** Convert non-essential possessions like electronics or collectibles into cash.
     - **Temporary Income Boost:** Seek temporary work, freelance gigs, or online jobs to supplement income.
3. **Utilizing Financial Assistance Programs:**

- ◦ **Government Support:**
    - ■ **Unemployment Benefits:** File for unemployment insurance if job loss is a factor.
    - ■ **Stimulus Packages and Tax Credits:** Monitor federal and state assistance programs for stimulus checks, tax credits, or low-interest emergency loans.
- ◦ **Community and Charitable Aid:**
    - ■ **Local Charities:** Research local food banks, utility assistance programs, and community groups offering support.
    - ■ **Financial Counseling Services:** Non-profit organizations provide free financial counseling to help people navigate debt and crisis management.

4. **Investment Adjustments:**
   - ◦ **Portfolio Diversification:**
       - ■ **Rebalance Investments:** Adjust asset allocation to diversify risk, shifting from volatile stocks to safer bonds or cash equivalents.
       - ■ **Alternative Investments:** Consider alternative investments that can hedge against market downturns, such as real estate or precious metals.
   - ◦ **Selling Underperforming Assets:**
       - ■ **Cutting Losses:** Avoid emotional attachment to underperforming investments and sell to limit further losses.

5. **Debt Management and Negotiation:**
   - ◦ **Credit Card Debt:**
       - ■ **Balance Transfer Cards:** Use balance transfer credit cards to move high-interest debt to low or zero-interest alternatives.
       - ■ **Direct Negotiation:** Contact creditors directly to negotiate lower interest rates or more manageable payment plans.
   - ◦ **Loan Restructuring:**

- **Student Loans:** Apply for income-driven repayment plans, deferments, or forbearance based on financial hardship.
- **Mortgage Refinancing:** Refinance existing mortgages at a lower interest rate or negotiate temporary forbearance.

6. **Developing a Long-Term Resilience Plan:**
   - **Building an Emergency Fund:**
       - **Gradual Savings Goals:** Aim to accumulate 3-6 months' worth of living expenses over time, prioritizing regular contributions to an emergency fund.
       - **High-Yield Accounts:** Store emergency funds in high-yield savings accounts for inflation-beating returns while maintaining liquidity.
   - **Diversifying Income Streams:**
       - **Side Hustles:** Develop side businesses that can offer steady income outside of regular employment.
       - **Passive Income:** Invest in income-generating assets like rental properties, dividend stocks, or digital products.

Maintaining a Positive Outlook During Tough Times:

1. **Stress Management Techniques:**
   - **Mindfulness Practices:**
       - **Meditation and Deep Breathing:** Reduce stress by dedicating time to guided meditation, deep breathing exercises, or yoga.
       - **Gratitude Journaling:** Reflect daily on positive aspects of life and accomplishments to shift focus away from financial pressures.
   - **Physical Exercise:**
       - **Routine Workouts:** Maintain a regular exercise schedule to boost mood and reduce anxiety, whether

through gym workouts, jogging, or home fitness routines.

- **Outdoor Activities:** Spend time outdoors walking, hiking, or cycling to reduce cabin fever and stimulate creativity.

2. **Support Networks:**
   - **Family and Friends:**
     - **Open Communication:** Share challenges and feelings with trusted friends and family members to receive emotional support and encouragement.
     - **Collaborative Solutions:** Engage in joint problem-solving with close ones to brainstorm strategies for managing financial issues collectively.
   - **Financial Advisors and Counselors:**
     - **Professional Guidance:** Work with financial advisors or counselors to create realistic plans that align with goals and available resources.
     - **Accountability Partners:** Stay accountable to goals by checking in with a trusted advisor or mentor regularly.

3. **Resilient Mindset:**
   - **Accepting Temporary Setbacks:**
     - **Perspective Shift:** View financial crises as opportunities for growth and learning rather than permanent failures.
     - **Self-Compassion:** Avoid self-criticism and practice compassion by recognizing that setbacks are temporary and normal during economic downturns.
   - **Goal Reassessment:**
     - **Flexible Goals:** Modify financial goals to fit new circumstances, setting attainable targets that can be gradually achieved.
     - **Focus on Progress:** Celebrate small wins and

incremental improvements to maintain motivation and reinforce positive behavior.

Conclusion: Managing financial crises requires both strategic planning and emotional resilience. By evaluating the current financial situation, taking immediate action steps, and creating long-term resilience plans, individuals can navigate downturns with confidence. A positive outlook and support network will help maintain mental well-being while pursuing gradual progress toward renewed financial stability.

Chapter 26: The Psychology of Money
How Emotions Affect Financial Decisions:

1. **Understanding Emotional Influence:**
   - **Emotional Bias in Decision-Making:**
     - **Anchoring Effect:** Relying heavily on the first piece of information received, which skews subsequent decisions even if the information is inaccurate.
     - **Herd Mentality:** Following the actions of others, especially during market bubbles or economic downturns, without individual critical analysis.
   - **Cognitive Dissonance:**
     - **Rationalization:** Justifying poor financial choices to align actions with desired beliefs, even when evidence contradicts them.
     - **Loss Aversion:** Fear of losing money leads to irrational decisions, such as holding onto losing investments or avoiding necessary risk-taking.
2. **Key Emotional Triggers:**
   - **Fear and Greed:**
     - **Fear of Missing Out (FOMO):** Drives speculative investment during market booms, often leading to buying at peak prices and significant losses when markets correct.
     - **Greed:** The desire for quick profits leads to impulsive decision-making and overextending financially, especially with high-risk investments.
   - **Stress and Anxiety:**
     - **Financial Anxiety:** Excessive worry about finances can lead to procrastination or avoidance, preventing people from addressing critical issues like debt management.
     - **Status Anxiety:** Comparing one's financial status

to others creates a pressure to overspend to "keep up," resulting in mounting debt and unsustainable lifestyles.

3. **Common Behavioral Patterns:**
   - **Overconfidence:**
     - **Overestimation:** Believing in one's financial acumen without sufficient data, often leading to risky trading and investment practices.
     - **Confirmation Bias:** Seeking information that aligns with pre-existing beliefs while ignoring conflicting evidence, reinforcing poor decisions.
   - **Mental Accounting:**
     - **Compartmentalization:** Treating money differently based on its source, like spending windfall gains frivolously while being frugal with earned income.
     - **Sunk Cost Fallacy:** Continuing with unprofitable projects because of prior investments rather than cutting losses.

Techniques for Maintaining Mental Health While Pursuing Wealth:

1. **Emotional Intelligence and Self-Awareness:**
   - **Recognizing Emotional Triggers:**
     - **Self-Reflection:** Regularly evaluate one's feelings before making significant financial decisions to ensure they align with long-term goals.
     - **Pause and Analyze:** Delay decisions during periods of heightened emotions like stress or excitement to prevent irrational behavior.
   - **Understanding Behavioral Patterns:**
     - **Journaling:** Track spending habits, investment choices, and the underlying emotions to identify patterns and address problematic behaviors.

- **Mindfulness Practices:** Use meditation or mindfulness techniques to stay grounded, helping individuals remain rational despite market volatility or financial stress.

2. **Cognitive Behavioral Techniques:**
   - **Reframing Financial Goals:**
     - **SMART Goals:** Set goals that are Specific, Measurable, Achievable, Relevant, and Time-bound to remain focused and motivated.
     - **Positive Visualization:** Visualize achieving financial goals to reinforce positive emotions and counter anxiety and fear.
   - **Challenge Cognitive Distortions:**
     - **All-or-Nothing Thinking:** Avoid viewing situations in extremes like "total success" or "total failure" and seek balanced, realistic assessments.
     - **Catastrophizing:** Stop imagining worst-case scenarios and instead develop contingency plans that address realistic risks.

3. **Building a Resilient Mindset:**
   - **Gratitude Practice:**
     - **Daily Reflections:** Reflect daily on achievements and positive aspects of financial progress to shift focus away from perceived shortcomings.
     - **Celebrate Milestones:** Recognize even small financial wins to reinforce positive behavior and maintain motivation.
   - **Adaptability:**
     - **Flexible Planning:** Prepare to adjust financial strategies based on changing circumstances without feeling like plans have "failed."
     - **Learning from Mistakes:** Treat financial missteps as learning experiences and adjust strategies accordingly.

4. **Support Systems and Accountability:**

- ◦ **Trusted Advisors:**
  - ■ **Financial Mentors:** Seek guidance from trusted mentors or advisors who can offer objective perspectives on financial decisions.
  - ■ **Therapeutic Support:** Work with financial therapists or counselors to address emotional challenges like anxiety or compulsive spending.
- ◦ **Community and Networks:**
  - ■ **Accountability Partners:** Partner with friends, family, or financial groups that align with one's goals and can offer support and constructive feedback.
  - ■ **Educational Networks:** Join financial literacy groups or communities to continue learning and share insights with others.

Conclusion: Financial decisions are deeply influenced by emotions, often leading to irrational behavior that can derail even the most well-thought-out plans. By understanding these emotional triggers and employing techniques like emotional intelligence, cognitive behavioral strategies, and resilient mindsets, individuals can minimize the impact of emotions and maintain mental health while pursuing wealth. Building supportive networks and practicing self-awareness are crucial steps to long-term financial success and personal fulfillment.

Chapter 27: Learning from Failures
Stories of Financial Setbacks and Comebacks:

1. **The Entrepreneur's Journey:**
   - **From Bankruptcy to Booming Business:**
     - **Initial Failure:** An entrepreneur who took out significant loans to start a brick-and-mortar retail business faced bankruptcy due to unforeseen market shifts and high overhead costs.
     - **The Turnaround:** After liquidation, they pivoted to online retail, utilizing knowledge gained from the first venture and cutting operational expenses. They rebuilt the brand into a thriving e-commerce business, focusing on a more profitable niche.
     - **Key Takeaways:**
       - **Agility:** Quickly adapting to market changes is crucial, especially with changing consumer behaviors.
       - **Lean Operations:** Reducing unnecessary expenses keeps businesses afloat during uncertain times.
2. **The Over-Leveraged Investor:**
   - **Real Estate Crash and Recovery:**
     - **Initial Failure:** An investor who relied heavily on leverage to expand their real estate portfolio suffered significant losses during the housing market crash, resulting in a high debt burden.
     - **The Turnaround:** They strategically divested underperforming properties and diversified their portfolio with commercial real estate and income-generating

assets. With prudent financial management and re-investment, they recovered and built a more stable investment strategy.

- **Key Takeaways:**
  - **Diversification:** Investing across different asset classes reduces risk exposure.
  - **Risk Assessment:** Regularly reassessing the investment strategy ensures alignment with market conditions.

3. **The Impulsive Spender:**
   - **Debt Spiral and Financial Literacy:**
     - **Initial Failure:** A professional who earned a high salary indulged in impulsive spending, accumulating debt on credit cards and personal loans until it became unmanageable.
     - **The Turnaround:** They sought financial counseling, created a strict budget, and negotiated debt repayment plans. By understanding personal finance better, they eventually eliminated their debt and built an emergency fund.
     - **Key Takeaways:**
       - **Financial Education:** Understanding the implications of debt is vital to avoid excessive borrowing.
       - **Accountability:** Working with advisors or accountability partners reinforces positive spending habits.

4. **The Serial Entrepreneur:**
   - **Tech Startup to Investment Success:**
     - **Initial Failure:** A tech entrepreneur launched multiple unsuccessful startups, each suffering from market misalignment and unsustainable growth strategies.
     - **The Turnaround:** They focused on learning from past failures, understanding market demand deeply,

and applying agile management strategies. Eventually, their fifth venture gained traction, achieved profitability, and attracted investor interest. They diversified into early-stage investments and helped guide new startups.

- **Key Takeaways:**
    - **Market Research:** Thorough market analysis reduces misalignment with consumer needs.
    - **Persistence:** Perseverance and willingness to iterate are essential when pursuing innovative business models.

Lessons on Resilience and Persistence:

1. **Embrace Failure as Learning:**
   - **Analyzing Setbacks:**
       - **Root Cause Analysis:** Instead of dwelling on failure emotionally, assess the core reasons and patterns that led to setbacks.
       - **Knowledge Application:** Apply insights gained from analysis to refine strategies, whether in personal finance, business, or investments.
   - **Cultivating Curiosity:**
       - **Growth Mindset:** Shift the mindset to view challenges as opportunities to improve and expand knowledge.
       - **Continuous Learning:** Invest in continuous financial education to enhance literacy and decision-making skills.
2. **Build a Resilience Framework:**
   - **Diversification:**
       - **Portfolio Mix:** Maintain a diversified portfolio that can withstand market volatility, combining stable and growth assets.

- **Income Streams:** Develop multiple income streams to buffer against unexpected economic downturns.
- **Safety Nets:**
  - **Emergency Fund:** Prioritize building an emergency fund that can cover living expenses for several months.
  - **Insurance:** Secure adequate insurance coverage, including health, property, and liability insurance, to minimize financial vulnerability.

3. **Seek Support Networks:**
   - **Mentorship and Coaching:**
     - **Financial Mentors:** Learn from experienced mentors who can offer unbiased advice on challenges and pitfalls.
     - **Peer Networks:** Join peer networks that encourage sharing of ideas and support through accountability.
   - **Professional Guidance:**
     - **Financial Advisors:** Utilize advisors to develop customized strategies aligned with goals.
     - **Counseling Services:** Seek counseling when financial stress leads to mental health issues, ensuring the emotional strength to recover.

4. **Stay Persistent:**
   - **Goal Setting:**
     - **SMART Goals:** Set Specific, Measurable, Achievable, Relevant, and Time-bound goals that motivate and inspire continued progress.
     - **Incremental Milestones:** Celebrate small wins along the way to avoid feeling overwhelmed by the larger objective.
   - **Adaptability:**
     - **Flexible Planning:** Be prepared to adapt plans and strategies when goals become unattainable due to changing conditions.
     - **Long-Term Vision:** Stay focused on long-term goals

despite short-term setbacks, maintaining optimism for a prosperous future.

Conclusion: Failures can act as catalysts for growth if they are approached with the right mindset. By analyzing setbacks, building resilience frameworks, and developing strong support networks, individuals can transform adversity into opportunities for personal and financial development. Persistence, adaptability, and continuous learning will ensure a solid foundation for achieving financial freedom, no matter how many setbacks are encountered along the way.

Chapter 28: 30-Day Challenge to Kickstart Your Financial Freedom

Daily Activities and Challenges to Improve Financial Health:

1. **Days 1-7: Laying the Foundation**
   - **Day 1: Self-Assessment**
     - **Activity:** Review your current financial status by listing your assets, liabilities, income, and expenses. Understand your net worth and categorize debts.
     - **Challenge:** Identify 2-3 areas where you are overspending or under-saving and commit to improvement.
   - **Day 2: Financial Education**
     - **Activity:** Research financial terms and strategies that you are unfamiliar with or that can enhance your knowledge (e.g., compound interest, diversified investments).
     - **Challenge:** Take notes on how these concepts apply to your personal situation.
   - **Day 3: Goal Setting**
     - **Activity:** Establish SMART financial goals that are Specific, Measurable, Achievable, Relevant, and Time-bound.
     - **Challenge:** Create a vision board to visualize your financial goals or write them down and place them where you will see them daily.
   - **Day 4: Creating a Budget**
     - **Activity:** Draft a monthly budget that realistically aligns with your income and planned expenses.
     - **Challenge:** Identify unnecessary expenses and set limits on discretionary spending.

- **Day 5: Building an Emergency Fund**
  - **Activity:** Start saving towards an emergency fund that can cover 3-6 months of living expenses.
  - **Challenge:** Deposit a small amount today and set up automatic transfers to continue contributing consistently.
- **Day 6: Analyzing Debts**
  - **Activity:** List all outstanding debts, including their interest rates and minimum payments.
  - **Challenge:** Choose a debt repayment strategy (e.g., avalanche or snowball) to prioritize your repayments.
- **Day 7: Financial Tools and Tracking**
  - **Activity:** Explore budgeting tools and apps that track spending and help meet savings goals.
  - **Challenge:** Download and set up an app to begin monitoring daily transactions.

2. **Days 8-14: Increasing Income Streams**
- **Day 8: Freelance Exploration**
  - **Activity:** Identify skills that can be offered as freelance services and research the demand for them.
  - **Challenge:** Set up a profile on a freelancing platform and apply for at least one gig.
- **Day 9: Monetizing Hobbies**
  - **Activity:** List hobbies or passions that have potential for commercialization, such as writing, crafting, or fitness.
  - **Challenge:** Develop a simple business plan for one hobby, outlining how to generate income.
- **Day 10: Digital Products**
  - **Activity:** Learn about creating digital products like e-books, online courses, or software.
  - **Challenge:** Outline a topic or product idea and start drafting the structure or prototype.
- **Day 11: Investment Portfolio Review**

- **Activity:** Review your investment portfolio, if applicable, and assess its diversification across different asset classes.
- **Challenge:** Research and identify at least two new investment opportunities that fit your risk tolerance.

- **Day 12: Real Estate Investigation**
  - **Activity:** Learn about real estate investment strategies (rental income, house flipping, REITs).
  - **Challenge:** Research your local real estate market and note potential investment opportunities.

- **Day 13: Passive Income Ideas**
  - **Activity:** Explore passive income opportunities such as affiliate marketing, royalties, or peer-to-peer lending.
  - **Challenge:** Choose one opportunity and develop a simple action plan.

- **Day 14: Networking for Growth**
  - **Activity:** Join an online or local financial network or community to exchange knowledge.
  - **Challenge:** Participate in a discussion, webinar, or forum to gain new insights.

3. **Days 15-21: Debt Reduction and Financial Optimization**
  - **Day 15: Credit Score Check**
    - **Activity:** Review your credit report and check your credit score.
    - **Challenge:** Identify inaccuracies or areas of improvement to boost your score.
  - **Day 16: Debt Repayment Plan**
    - **Activity:** Implement your chosen debt repayment strategy and automate payments where possible.
    - **Challenge:** Negotiate lower interest rates or better payment terms with your creditors.
  - **Day 17: Insurance Audit**

- **Activity:** Review your insurance policies for gaps or overlapping coverage.
- **Challenge:** Adjust policies to eliminate wasteful premiums and ensure proper protection.

- **Day 18: Tax Planning**
    - **Activity:** Identify deductions or credits applicable to your financial situation and research tax-saving strategies.
    - **Challenge:** Start organizing tax documents to simplify preparation and maximize returns.

- **Day 19: Financial Advisor Consultation**
    - **Activity:** Seek advice from a certified financial advisor for an objective review of your financial plans.
    - **Challenge:** Create a list of questions or concerns to discuss during the consultation.

- **Day 20: Lifestyle Optimization**
    - **Activity:** Reevaluate discretionary expenses like subscriptions or memberships to find areas for reduction.
    - **Challenge:** Cancel at least one subscription or membership that doesn't align with your goals.

- **Day 21: Resilient Financial Mindset**
    - **Activity:** Reflect on your financial journey so far and identify emotional triggers that affect financial decisions.
    - **Challenge:** Practice mindfulness techniques or write affirmations to build a positive and resilient mindset.

4. **Days 22-30: Tracking Progress and Adjusting Goals**
    - **Day 22: Progress Evaluation**
        - **Activity:** Compare your financial situation to Day 1 and note changes or improvements.
        - **Challenge:** Adjust goals or strategies if needed, based on current progress.
    - **Day 23: Budget Refinement**

- **Activity:** Review your monthly budget with new insights and refine it further to enhance savings.
- **Challenge:** Allocate additional funds toward savings or investments.

- **Day 24: Income Stream Enhancement**
  - **Activity:** Evaluate your new income streams or ideas for feasibility and profitability.
  - **Challenge:** Adjust your approach or marketing strategy to enhance profitability.

- **Day 25: Investment Strategy Adjustment**
  - **Activity:** Review your investment strategy with market trends in mind and rebalance your portfolio if necessary.
  - **Challenge:** Add a new asset or diversify holdings for better risk management.

- **Day 26: Financial Support System**
  - **Activity:** Strengthen relationships with mentors, financial advisors, or peers who provide support and accountability.
  - **Challenge:** Share your progress with them and seek feedback or advice.

- **Day 27: Resilience Plan**
  - **Activity:** Develop a contingency plan to manage potential financial crises or setbacks.
  - **Challenge:** Create a backup income source or emergency contact list.

- **Day 28: Refining Daily Habits**
  - **Activity:** Identify unproductive financial habits that emerged during the challenge.
  - **Challenge:** Replace at least one with a productive habit, like daily expense tracking.

- **Day 29: Celebration and Reflection**
  - **Activity:** Celebrate your successes, even small ones, and reflect on your growth and lessons learned.

- **Challenge:** Treat yourself within budget to reinforce positive financial behavior.
- **Day 30: Future Planning**
    - **Activity:** Review long-term financial goals and how the 30-day challenge aligns with them.
    - **Challenge:** Draft a new 30-day challenge to continue your journey to financial freedom.

Tracking Progress and Adjusting Goals:

1. **Tracking Tools:**
    - **Financial Software or Apps:** Utilize financial tracking tools for seamless monitoring of progress across different goals.
    - **Manual Logs:** Maintain a journal to capture daily progress, challenges, and reflections for personal analysis.
2. **Regular Evaluations:**
    - **Weekly Reviews:** Conduct a weekly review of progress and recalibrate goals based on achievements and challenges.
    - **Monthly Assessments:** Schedule a comprehensive financial assessment at the end of each month to evaluate broader goals.
3. **Adjusting Goals:**
    - **Flexible Goal-Setting:** Be willing to refine goals based on changing circumstances and financial realities.
    - **Incremental Milestones:** Break down larger goals into achievable milestones to maintain motivation and direction.
4. **Accountability Partners:**
    - **Peer Support:** Share your goals and progress with accountability partners to gain support and objective feedback.
    - **Professional Advisors:** Consult with financial advisors for expert insights on further improving strategies and goals.

Conclusion: The 30-Day Challenge offers a structured approach to kickstarting your journey to financial freedom. By setting specific daily activities, tracking progress, and adjusting goals, you'll develop healthy financial habits and a resilient mindset. This challenge lays the groundwork for a proactive financial strategy, empowering you to achieve and maintain long-term prosperity.

Chapter 29: Networking and Mentoring
How to Find and Work with a Mentor

1. **The Importance of Mentorship:**
   - **Guidance and Wisdom:** A mentor provides valuable insight and advice based on their personal experiences and professional journey, helping mentees avoid common pitfalls and seize promising opportunities.
   - **Accountability and Support:** Regular check-ins with a mentor can encourage consistent progress, keeping mentees aligned with their goals.

2. **Identifying the Right Mentor:**
   - **Clarify Your Objectives:** Before searching for a mentor, clearly define your goals. Do you need help with entrepreneurship, investment strategies, or career development?
   - **Research and Seek Recommendations:** Explore your industry's leaders or ask colleagues and professionals for mentor recommendations. Look for individuals who have excelled in areas aligned with your objectives.
   - **Evaluate Compatibility:** An ideal mentor should align with your values, communication style, and vision. A compatible mentor-mentee relationship fosters trust and effective guidance.

3. **Approaching Potential Mentors:**
   - **Be Genuine and Clear:** When reaching out, express genuine admiration for their achievements and convey clear expectations. Explain why you think their expertise is valuable and how you would benefit from their mentorship.
   - **Offer Value:** Show how you can contribute to the mentor-mentee relationship. Whether through thoughtful questions, research assistance, or referrals, offering value can foster a balanced partnership.

4. **Maintaining a Productive Mentor-Mentee Relationship:**
   - **Establish Clear Expectations:** Early in the relationship, define the mentor's role, preferred communication methods, and meeting frequency.
   - **Prepare for Meetings:** Come prepared with specific questions or challenges to maximize each interaction and demonstrate your commitment to growth.
   - **Act on Feedback:** Show appreciation for their advice by implementing their suggestions, then follow up with progress updates to reinforce that their guidance is impactful.

5. **Transitioning or Ending Mentorship:**
   - **Natural Progression:** A mentorship relationship may evolve over time. Acknowledge this progression and explore how the mentor can continue providing value in new areas.
   - **Gratitude and Closure:** If the relationship naturally ends or isn't meeting your needs, thank the mentor for their time and support. Express gratitude and offer to maintain a positive professional connection.

Building a Network for Business and Investment Opportunities

1. **The Value of Networking:**
   - **Information and Insights:** A strong network provides access to industry trends, investment opportunities, and potential partnerships.
   - **Collaboration and Support:** Networking fosters collaboration and builds a supportive community of like-minded professionals who can exchange knowledge and resources.

2. **Developing a Strategic Networking Plan:**
   - **Define Objectives:** Be clear on what you aim to achieve through networking, such as finding investors, expanding your client base, or gaining industry insights.
   - **Identify Key Contacts:** List professionals who could help

you meet your objectives, such as potential partners, clients, investors, or advisors.

- **Choose Effective Platforms:** Select networking channels that align with your goals, like conferences, professional associations, or online groups.

3. **Networking Techniques:**
   - **Elevator Pitch:** Prepare a concise, compelling pitch that introduces your background, goals, and value proposition in under a minute.
   - **Active Listening:** Listen attentively to others' stories and goals, ask thoughtful questions, and respond empathetically. This builds genuine connections.
   - **Follow Up and Stay Engaged:** After meeting new contacts, follow up with personalized messages or value-driven insights to sustain the connection.

4. **Leveraging Online Networks:**
   - **Professional Social Media:** Maintain an active presence on LinkedIn, Twitter, or other relevant platforms, sharing valuable content to showcase your expertise and attract like-minded individuals.
   - **Industry-Specific Forums:** Participate in niche forums or groups where you can exchange knowledge with peers and learn about emerging trends or business opportunities.

5. **Expanding Your Reach:**
   - **Attend Networking Events:** Engage in webinars, seminars, or mixers hosted by industry groups to meet diverse professionals.
   - **Host Your Own Events:** Organize webinars, workshops, or meetups where you can share your expertise while fostering collaboration among participants.
   - **Provide Referrals and Support:** Building goodwill by referring clients or sharing resources strengthens your reputation and encourages reciprocity.

6. **Maintaining Long-Term Relationships:**

- **Regular Check-ins:** Periodically touch base with key contacts to maintain rapport and exchange updates on achievements, challenges, or market trends.
- **Offer Value Consistently:** Share useful insights, resources, or opportunities that align with their interests or goals.
- **Be Authentic and Supportive:** Show genuine interest in their success and provide encouragement or assistance where possible.

Conclusion: Networking and mentoring play crucial roles in achieving financial freedom. While mentors offer personalized guidance to navigate challenges, a well-connected network provides information, collaboration, and support that can open new doors. By finding the right mentors, implementing effective networking strategies, and maintaining long-term relationships, you can build a powerful support system that accelerates your journey toward prosperity.

Chapter 30: Continual Learning and Skill Development
Importance of Lifelong Learning in Financial Success

1. **Adapting to a Changing World:**
   - **Technological Advancements:** Rapid technological progress continuously reshapes industries and job markets, requiring new skills for emerging opportunities.
   - **Economic Shifts:** Globalization and evolving economic conditions impact industries differently, making it crucial to diversify your skill set to remain adaptable and relevant.
2. **Mindset for Lifelong Learning:**
   - **Growth vs. Fixed Mindset:** Adopting a growth mindset helps individuals view challenges as learning opportunities rather than obstacles.
   - **Self-Assessment:** Regularly evaluate your skills and knowledge to identify gaps and areas for improvement.
3. **Financial Literacy and New Opportunities:**
   - **Investment Strategies:** Advanced understanding of investment principles, such as index funds, retirement accounts, or alternative assets, can unlock significant financial growth.
   - **Entrepreneurial Mindset:** Learning entrepreneurial strategies can help turn ideas into profitable businesses, expanding income streams beyond traditional employment.
   - **Tax Efficiency:** Staying informed on tax laws and strategies ensures optimal planning to reduce liabilities and boost after-tax returns.
4. **Career Growth:**
   - **Professional Development:** Advanced certifications, degrees, and specialized courses can increase qualifications, leading to higher salaries or promotions.
   - **Cross-Functional Skills:** Building complementary skills,

like coding, management, or marketing, enhances overall productivity and opens doors to new career paths.

Resources and Courses that Offer Valuable Skills

1. **Online Learning Platforms:**
    - **Massive Open Online Courses (MOOCs):** Websites like Coursera, edX, and Udemy offer thousands of courses from top universities and institutions. Topics range from finance and entrepreneurship to data science and digital marketing.
    - **Skill-Specific Sites:** Platforms such as LinkedIn Learning and Pluralsight provide curated courses tailored to industry needs, helping professionals upskill efficiently.
2. **Certifications and Designations:**
    - **Financial Certifications:** Earning credentials like Chartered Financial Analyst (CFA), Certified Financial Planner (CFP), or Financial Risk Manager (FRM) can significantly increase credibility and expertise.
    - **Industry-Specific Certifications:** Certifications in fields like IT (CompTIA, AWS), marketing (Google Analytics, HubSpot), or management (Project Management Professional) can enhance specialized knowledge.
3. **Books, Podcasts, and Articles:**
    - **Books on Financial Success:** Classic works like *Rich Dad Poor Dad*, *Your Money or Your Life*, or *The Intelligent Investor* offer foundational knowledge.
    - **Podcasts and Newsletters:** Following relevant podcasts like *The Tim Ferriss Show*, *BiggerPockets*, or *Smart Passive Income* and subscribing to industry newsletters keeps you updated on the latest insights and strategies.
4. **Workshops, Conferences, and Meetups:**
    - **Industry Conferences:** Participating in industry-specific events or international summits provides practical knowledge, networking opportunities, and inspiration.

- ○ **Workshops and Webinars:** Local business organizations or online webinars offer valuable, hands-on training for specific skills, such as investment analysis, negotiation, or coding.
5. **Mentorship and Coaching:**
   - ○ **Business Mentors:** A mentor offers personalized advice and insights into navigating professional challenges and expanding your network.
   - ○ **Personal Coaching:** Hiring a financial, life, or career coach provides accountability and helps align personal goals with effective strategies.

Conclusion: Continual learning is vital in achieving financial success. With the world constantly evolving, a commitment to expanding your skill set and knowledge is key to staying ahead and identifying new opportunities. By adopting a growth mindset and actively leveraging the wealth of educational resources available, you can build a robust foundation for long-term prosperity and adaptability in any economic landscape.

Chapter 31: Innovations in Finance: Fintech and Beyond
Overview of Emerging Financial Technologies

1. **Defining Fintech:**
   - **Concept and Evolution:** Fintech, short for financial technology, encompasses a broad range of innovations that streamline and transform financial services. Initially centered around online banking and payment apps, fintech now includes blockchain, robo-advisors, and machine learning applications.
   - **Key Drivers:** Advances in data analytics, cloud computing, and mobile technology have paved the way for fintech, improving efficiency, security, and accessibility.
2. **Major Innovations in Fintech:**
   - **Blockchain Technology:** Blockchain underpins cryptocurrencies like Bitcoin and Ethereum, enabling secure, decentralized transactions. Smart contracts built on blockchain platforms automate processes like cross-border payments and supply chain tracking.
   - **Robo-Advisors:** Automated financial advisors leverage algorithms to provide personalized investment recommendations and portfolio management at lower costs than traditional advisors.
   - **Peer-to-Peer Lending:** P2P platforms match borrowers with individual lenders, bypassing traditional banks and offering competitive interest rates for both parties.
   - **Insurtech:** Startups in insurance technology are modernizing the industry with digital platforms, behavioral data analysis, and personalized coverage plans.
   - **Open Banking:** Open banking allows third-party developers to securely access customer data from banks and payment

service providers through application programming interfaces (APIs), enabling personalized services and increased financial transparency.

- **Payment Innovations:** Contactless payments, digital wallets, and QR code systems make transactions faster and more convenient. Blockchain-based stablecoins offer an alternative to traditional payment systems.

How Fintech is Changing the Landscape of Personal Finance

1. **Accessibility and Inclusion:**
   - **Financial Inclusion:** Mobile banking apps and digital wallets provide basic financial services to unbanked or underbanked populations, enabling them to manage money, pay bills, and transfer funds easily.
   - **Lower Barriers to Investing:** Robo-advisors and micro-investing platforms offer entry-level investing opportunities with minimal fees and customizable risk levels.

2. **Efficiency and Convenience:**
   - **Automated Savings and Budgeting:** AI-powered tools analyze spending patterns and automatically save or invest funds, making it easier to stay on track with financial goals.
   - **Real-Time Monitoring:** Digital banking platforms offer real-time tracking of transactions, account balances, and credit scores, giving users instant insights into their financial health.

3. **Security and Fraud Prevention:**
   - **Biometric Authentication:** Fingerprint, facial recognition, and voice biometrics add layers of security to digital transactions and help prevent identity theft.
   - **AI Fraud Detection:** Advanced algorithms detect unusual patterns in transactions, flagging suspicious activities and reducing fraud risks.

4. **Personalized Financial Services:**

- **Customized Credit Scoring:** Alternative credit scoring models utilize social media, purchase history, and utility payments to provide credit access to those without conventional credit history.
- **Tailored Recommendations:** Data-driven insights enable fintech companies to recommend suitable financial products, whether for investments, loans, or insurance policies.

5. **Disrupting Traditional Banking Models:**
   - **Neobanks:** Digital-only banks operate with lower overhead costs, passing savings to customers through competitive fees and higher interest rates.
   - **Legacy Institutions Adapting:** Traditional banks are partnering with fintech startups or developing their own digital solutions to retain customers and compete in the evolving market.

Conclusion: The rapid rise of fintech is fundamentally altering how individuals interact with financial services. By increasing accessibility, streamlining processes, and offering tailored solutions, these innovations have empowered individuals to take greater control of their financial health. Understanding these emerging technologies is crucial for navigating this evolving landscape and seizing opportunities to grow and protect one's wealth in this digital age. As fintech continues to advance, those who adapt and embrace its potential will be better positioned to achieve financial freedom and prosperity.

<u>Message from the Author:</u>

I hope you enjoyed this book, I love astrology and knew there was not a book such as this out on the shelf. I love metaphysical items as well. Please check out my other books:

-Life of Government Benefits

-My life of Hell

-My life with Hydrocephalus

-Red Sky

-World Domination:Woman's rule

-World Domination:Woman's Rule 2: The War

-Life and Banishment of Apophis: book 1

-The Kidney Friendly Diet

-The Ultimate Hemp Cookbook

-Creating a Dispensary(legally)

-Cleanliness throughout life: the importance of showering from childhood to adulthood.

-Strong Roots: The Risks of Overcoddling children

-Hemp Horoscopes: Cosmic Insights and Earthly Healing

- Celestial Hemp Navigating the Zodiac: Through the Green Cosmos

-Astrological Hemp: Aligning The Stars with Earth's Ancient Herb

-The Astrological Guide to Hemp: Stars, Signs, and Sacred Leaves

-Green Growth: Innovative Marketing Strategies for your Hemp Products and Dispensary

-Cosmic Cannabis

-Astrological Munchies

-Henry The Hemp

-Zodiacal Roots: The Astrological Soul Of Hemp

- **Green Constellations: Intersection of Hemp and Zodiac**

-Hemp in The Houses: An astrological Adventure Through The Cannabis Galaxy

-Galactic Ganja Guide

Heavenly Hemp

Zodiac Leaves

Doctor Who Astrology

Cannastrology

Stellar Satvias and Cosmic Indicas

Celestial Cannabis: A Zodiac Journey

AstroHerbology: The Sky and The Soil: Volume 1

AstroHerbology:Celestial Cannabis:Volume 2

Cosmic Cannabis Cultivation

The Starry Guide to Herbal Harmony: Volume 1

The Starry Guide to Herbal Harmony: Cannabis Universe: Volume 2

Yugioh Astrology: Astrological Guide to Deck, Duels and more

Nightmare Mansion: Echoes of The Abyss

Nightmare Mansion 2: Legacy of Shadows

Nightmare Mansion 3: Shadows of the Forgotten

Nightmare Mansion 4: Echoes of the Damned

The Life and Banishment of Apophis: Book 2

Nightmare Mansion: Halls of Despair

Healing with Herb: Cannabis and Hydrocephalus

Planetary Pot: Aligning with Astrological Herbs: Volume 1

Fast Track to Freedom: 30 Days to Financial Independence Using AI, Assets, and Agile Hustles

Cosmic Hemp Pathways

Check out my Virtual dispensary for all your hemp needs: https://shift.store/sg1fan23477/retail

If you want solar for your home go here: https://www.harborsolar.live/apophisenterprises/

<u>**Instagrams:**</u>

@apophis_enterprises,

@hempkingdom2024,

@apophisbookemporium,

@apophisfashion,

@apophisscardshop

Twitter: @apophisenterpr1,

Tiktok:@apophisenterprise

Youtube: @sg1fan23477

Podcast: Apophis Chat Zone: https://open.spotify.com/show/5zXbrCLEV2xzCp8ybrfI1sk?si=fb4d4fdbdce44dec

Newsletter: https://apophiss-newsletter-27c897.beehiiv.com/

www.ingramcontent.com/pod-product-compliance
Lightning Source LLC
Chambersburg PA
CBHW061137160726
48006CB00038B/2125